MENTORING GUIDEBOOK

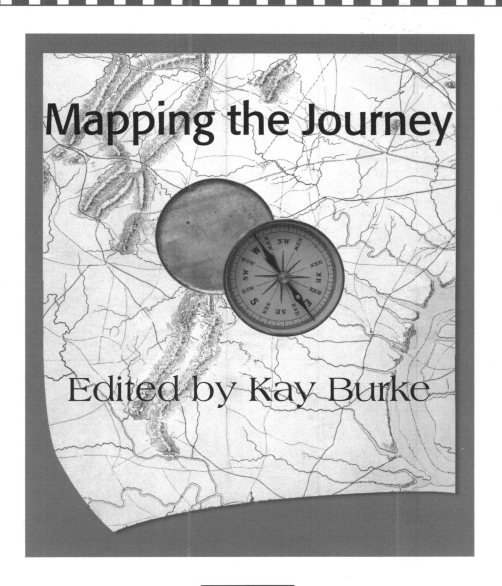

Mapping the Journey

Edited by Kay Burke

SkyLight
Professional
Development

Mentoring Guidebook: Mapping the Journey

Published by SkyLight Professional Development
2626 S. Clearbrook Dr., Arlington Heights, IL 60005
800-348-4474 or 847-290-6600
Fax 847-290-6609
info@skylightedu.com
http://www.skylightedu.com

President: Carol Luitjens
Executive Editor: Chris Jaeggi
Acquisitions Editor: Jean Ward
Editor: Anne Kaske
Editorial Coordinator: Donna Ramirez
Cover Designer and Illustrator: David Stockman
Book Designer: Bruce Leckie
Production Supervisor: Bob Crump

LCCCN 2001095303
ISBN 1-57517-546-0

3017-McN
Item Number 2410
ZYXWVUTSRQPONMLKJIHGFEDCBA
08 07 06 05 04 03 02 01   15 14 13 12 11 10 9 8 7 6 5 4 3 2 1

There are
one-story intellects,
two-story intellects, and
three-story intellects with skylights.

All fact collectors, who have no aim beyond their facts, are

one-story minds.

Two-story minds
compare, reason, generalize,
using the labors of the fact collectors
as well as their own.

Three-story minds
idealize, imagine, predict—their best illumination
comes from above,

through the **skylight**.

—Oliver Wendell Holmes

SkyLight
Professional
Development

Acknowledgments

SkyLight's mentoring journey began in January 2001 when Julie Sausen, Karen Evans, Vikki Myers, and I first met to discuss the essential skills we thought new teachers needed in order to become effective educators. The conversations continued as we worked with Carol Luitjens and the SkyLight team to launch our Mentoring Program, which now includes videotapes, distance learning courses, an annual conference, a training manual, practical research-based books, on-site trainings, and this guidebook. Julie and I worked closely with Chris Jaeggi, Anne Kaske, and Jean Ward in Publishing to select the key chapters from SkyLight books that we felt would provide essential skills beginning teachers need to succeed.

Contributors include Barry Sweeny, Debra Pitton, Jan Skowron, Jim Bellanca, and my own mentor, Robin Fogarty. *Mapping the Journey* is designed to show mentors how to help beginning teachers become competent and caring educators. Section I describes ways to structure a mentoring program and how to provide appropriate feedback and support. Section II provides strategies to help protégés plan basic lessons and integrated units, establish a positive classroom environment, teach and monitor social skills, and handle behavior problems. SkyLight's goal for this guidebook is to synthesize the most recent research on best practices in teaching and learning and to provide both mentors and protégés with user-friendly strategies to implement in their classrooms.

I would like to thank Bruce Leckie, David Stockman, Bob Crump, and Donna Ramirez in Publishing for their continued cooperation, creativity, and commitment throughout this project and all my other projects during my eleven years at SkyLight. I would especially like to thank Julie Sausen for her commitment to the program, Anne Kaske for her editing skills, and Susan Gray for her multi-tasking abilities during the "Mentor Madness Months."

Finally, all of us at SkyLight would like to thank mentor teachers throughout the world for their willingness to share their expertise, time, and enthusiasm with the ever-increasing number of beginning teachers. Their commitment to support and nurture new teachers not only enhances the profession, but also improves education for all students.

—KAY BURKE
September 2001

Contents

Introduction

Beginning teachers who do not participate in an Induction Program are twice as likely to leave as those who do participate. (NEA *Today,* Vol. 19, No. 8, May 2001)

he journey new teachers embark upon when they enter the educational profession offers exciting challenges that stimulate personal growth. The adrenaline flows when a first-year teacher encounters her first group of students without being under the watchful eyes of the supervising teacher sitting quietly in the back of the room. New teachers quickly realize, however, that they must take control of the classroom and make hundreds of decisions affecting the lives of the children entrusted to their care. Even though many first-year teachers have observed other teachers and experienced student teaching in college, the academic and classroom management challenges faced by first-year educators can be overwhelming. According to statistics from the National Education Association (NEA), 30 percent of new teachers leave within the first five years! In big cities, the percentage leaving within the first five years is even higher: 50 percent.

In some schools new teachers are assigned a "buddy" teacher to show them around the school and help them get their books and supplies. Often, the buddies teach the same grade level or content area so they also help the new teacher plan their curriculum. Usually the arrangement is informal and neither party receives any official training.

A more formal type of mentoring program may be required, however, because of the retirement of so many Baby Boomer generation educators and the subsequent need to recruit and train new teachers to fill growing numbers of vacancies.

Statisticians predict a need to hire 0.5 million to 2.5 million new teachers over the next decade. In addition to teacher retirements, the demand for so many new teachers is the result of the increasing numbers of students and the call for class-size reduction programs (Schultz as cited in Scherer 1999, p. 99). Recruiting, training, and retaining qualified teachers are important priorities in many cities as districts struggle to hire certified teachers and to attract people from business and overseas to fill teaching vacancies. Schools and districts across the country are creating or expanding formal mentoring programs to help new educators become committed, competent, and confident professionals who enjoy teaching.

The term *mentoring* comes from classical literature. In the Greek epic, the *Odyssey,* the poet Homer describes how the young hero Odysseus gave the responsibility of raising his son, Telemachus, to Mentor, his trusted friend and advisor, before he sailed to Troy to fight in the Trojan War. Mentor guided Telemachus while Odysseus was away by educating him in all of the physical, social, and intellectual facets of life. When Odysseus returned to Ithaca after ten years of fighting the Trojan war and ten years of wandering in search of his homeland, Telemachus had grown into an independent thinker who readily helped his father reclaim his property and rescue his wife from ambitious suitors.

The term *mentor* today usually refers to someone with more experience who teaches someone with less experience. The person with less experience could be called a *mentee,* a *beginning teacher,* a *novice,* or a *protégé.* Protégé is derived from a French term and means "one who is protected . . . by a person with experience, prominence, or influence" (Merriam-Webster's Collegiate Dictionary, Tenth ed.).

Just as Mentor assisted young Telemachus on his life's journey, so too do mentor teachers assist new teachers as they begin their teaching careers. The excerpts in this book provide critical components mentors can use to help their protégés gain confidence in their teaching and develop trust in their mentor relationship. This book also provides important concepts and lessons to help educators shape the social and academic lives of their students. Mentoring is a process that requires dedication, commitment, and an openness to a trusting,

The articles in this book provide key components for mentors to help their protégés gain confidence in their teaching and develop trust in the mentoring process.

ongoing relationship on the part of both the mentor and the protégé. One goal of any mentoring program is to empower veteran teachers to become skillful coaches who help beginning educators gain confidence in their abilities to meet the diverse needs of their students. I hope this guidebook will help map the journey toward providing a positive and stimulating learning environment for the mentors, protégés, and students.

REFERENCES

Merriam-Webster's Collegiate® Dictionary, Tenth Edition. 1996. Springfield, MA: Merriam-Webster, Incorporated.

National Education Association. *A better beginning: Helping new teachers survive and thrive.* A guide for NEA local affiliates interested in creating new teacher support systems. A publication of the NEA New Teacher Support Initiative. Washington, DC: National Education Association.

NEA Today. 2001. Young, dedicated—and out the door. *NEA Today.* 19(8). <www.nea.org/neatoday>

Schultz, B. 1999. Combining mentoring and assessment in California. In *A better beginning: Supporting and mentoring new teachers,* edited by M. Scherer. Alexandria, VA: Association for Supervision and Curriculum Development.

Setting the Course

Jan—
These techniques work
great in class. Let's
get together next week
and talk!

Sharon

Janice Langley
234 S. Cedar St.
Minton, VT 02234

Teaching is an unusual profession because the first-year teacher in most cases is assigned to the same tasks in and out of the classroom as a long-term veteran (Heidkamp and Shapiro 1999, p. 41).

Before embarking on a journey, it is always helpful to meet and get to know one's traveling companions. Schools and school districts engage in a wide variety of formal and informal social activities before school starts to help the seasoned travelers, the mentors, work with the first-time travelers, the protégés, to set the course for the new school year. Sometimes the activities are very structured and form the basis of the first steps in a formal two-to-three year new teacher induction program. The formal induction program may include an orientation program, professional development trainings, mentor training, peer support groups, classroom observations, professional development plans, and a professional portfolio.

In Selection 1, Barry Sweeny shows how all the puzzle pieces of an induction program fit together to form a coherent and integrated long-term development program to initiate new teachers. He defines a common vocabulary for all involved in the process and provides guidance in deciding whether to take an informal approach to mentoring beginning teachers or to establish a formal mentoring program to ensure more accountability.

Sweeny defines the roles of the mentor and the evolving picture of the protégé. He also describes the differences between the traditional one-to-one mentoring relationship and the team approach where a group of teachers shares the mentoring duties and their multiple talents and strengths with the protégé. Based upon his extensive experience working with mentoring programs, he includes checklists to cover many first and second-week responsibilities of new teachers.

In Selection 2, Debra Pitton continues the discussion by addressing the needs of the mentee (i.e., protégé) as well as the expectations for both mentors and mentees. She feels it is critical to have the mentor provide a mirror to allow new teachers to get an accurate image of what is happening in their classrooms. The observations and guiding questions can help the mentee recognize the need for some action or change. The

By working together to set the course, mentors and protégés forge a strong foundation.

feedback conversations and the questions to extend thinking and reflection provide powerful learning tools for the beginning teacher.

In Selection 3, Debra Pitton reviews what she calls the "heart of mentoring"—the necessity of open communications. Both verbal and nonverbal signals should provide nonjudgmental feedback that allows the mentee to discover and solve problems independently whenever possible.

Sometimes, however, the mentor may have to intervene in order to prevent serious problems that could jeopardize the students' learning or safety. A trial and error approach to teaching is not always in the best interest of the students. Therefore, the mentor has to know how to be the "guide on the side" and how to offer suggestions in a supportive way, especially if the situation requires immediate action.

Section I, Setting the Course, focuses on the initial stages of helping mentors and protégés become familiar and comfortable with the mentoring process. Together the mentors and the new teachers define their respective roles and develop a common vocabulary to help them communicate effectively. Mentors and protégés who take the time to define their responsibilities and share their expectations for the partnership create a strong foundation for future growth. Defining the ground rules for mentoring helps set the course for a positive and mutually beneficial mentoring relationship. Each journey begins with one step and most new teachers look forward to the new adventure. Proactive educators, however, spend time planning the trip in order to avoid unpleasant surprises or unexpected diversions. By working together to set the course before the first day of school, mentors and protégés forge a strong foundation for building a successful mentoring experience.

The mentor has to know how to be the "guide on the side" and how to offer suggestions in a supportive way.

REFERENCE

Heidkamp, A. and J. Shapiro. 1999. The elements of a supportive induction program. In *A better beginning: supporting and mentoring new teachers,* edited by M. Scherer. Alexandria, VA: Association for Supervision and Curriculum Development.

More and more states have mandated mentoring programs for all new teachers. Sweeny reviews the issues leaders need to address in order to meet the needs of the new teachers and the districts.

Structures for Induction and Mentoring Programs

by **Barry Sweeny**

This selection explores some fundamental issues program leaders must consider sooner or later in a mentoring program. Some of the issues discussed regard how leaders intend the individuals in the program to think about mentoring. The other issues concern decisions about program-level strategies that determine how leaders should conduct the program. Figure 1.1 defines the terms used throughout Selection 1. Figure 1.2 outlines the components of a teacher induction program. Although this selection primarily focuses on the mentoring piece of the puzzle, it is helpful to understand how mentoring can fit into a complete induction program.

Informal or Formal Mentoring?

Veteran teachers are usually very helpful and supportive people. However, beginning educators can easily fall through the cracks despite others' informal intentions to be helpful, especially once the school year has started and the pace of activity has accelerated to

Adapted from *Leading the Teacher Induction and Mentoring Program* by B. Sweeny, pp. xii, xiii, 1–14. © 2001 by SkyLight Training and Publishing.

Common Vocabulary for Uncommon Roles

1. **Beginning Educator**—A brand new educator who has little or no previous paid experience as an educator.

2. **New Educator**—An educator with at least two or more years of paid professional education experience, but who is newly hired in the district.

3. **Protégé**—A beginning or new educator who is working with a mentor.

4. **Mentor**—The title and status applied to a person who assumes the primary responsibility to provide mentoring. The mentor is a more experienced and, frequently, more senior person who works in a similar location and role as the protégé.

5. **Mentoring**—The complex developmental process mentors use to support and guide their protégés through the necessary transitions that are a part of learning how to be effective educators and career-long learners.

6. **Team Mentoring**—An approach to mentoring that divides the tasks of mentoring among several veteran educators who share the responsibilities based on their individual strengths. A teacher who has excellent, engaging lessons can help a protégé in a different way than can a teacher whose strength is avoiding and defusing confrontations in the classroom. Each contributes in different ways to the development and support of the protégé.

7. **Induction**—The activities and processes necessary to successfully induct a novice teacher into the profession. An effective induction program should include orientation, mentoring, staff development specific to the protégé's needs, observations of experienced teachers at work, and peer support groups.

8. **Coaching**—The support for learning provided by a colleague who uses observation, data collection, and descriptive, nonjudgmental reporting on specific requested behaviors and technical skills. The goal is to help an individual see his or her own patterns of behavior through someone else's eyes and to prompt reflection, goal-setting, and action to increase the desired results.

Figure 1.1

The Components of an Effective Induction Program

Figuring out the pieces you need to make an effective induction program should not be a puzzle. All you need is the lid for the box of puzzle pieces so you can see how to fit them all together effectively. Once you have the big picture, you can do it!

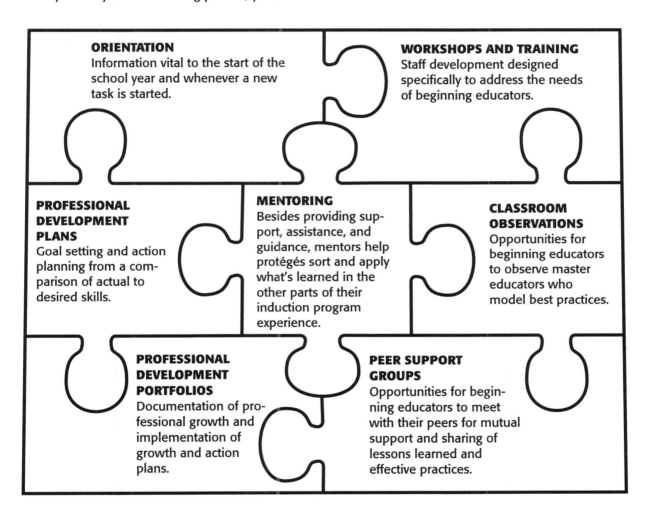

ORIENTATION
Information vital to the start of the school year and whenever a new task is started.

WORKSHOPS AND TRAINING
Staff development designed specifically to address the needs of beginning educators.

PROFESSIONAL DEVELOPMENT PLANS
Goal setting and action planning from a comparison of actual to desired skills.

MENTORING
Besides providing support, assistance, and guidance, mentors help protégés sort and apply what's learned in the other parts of their induction program experience.

CLASSROOM OBSERVATIONS
Opportunities for beginning educators to observe master educators who model best practices.

PROFESSIONAL DEVELOPMENT PORTFOLIOS
Documentation of professional growth and implementation of growth and action plans.

PEER SUPPORT GROUPS
Opportunities for beginning educators to meet with their peers for mutual support and sharing of lessons learned and effective practices.

Figure 1.2

what is typical for September. This can occur because everyone who would like to help the beginning teacher becomes extremely busy with his or her own work, and because some may fear appearing critical of the beginning teacher's work and thus are uncomfortable making suggestions or offering help.

In addition, beginning teachers often have so much to learn and to do immediately at the start of their new jobs, they may find it difficult to take time out from their work to seek out the assistance they need. They frequently believe they are expected to do the same work as a twenty-year veteran, and because of this they often do not want to reveal their concerns and problems for fear of looking incompetent.

Most school districts care about the success of their new employees and the students they serve. Many educational leaders have become dissatisfied with the informal approach to mentoring beginning teachers. Leaders who want to ensure beginning teacher success often find that an informal approach makes it difficult to know whether a given person is receiving the help he or she needs, and which experienced teachers are really helping their new colleagues and therefore deserve support or some form of recognition.

Another factor causing the move to a more formal mentoring approach is the increasing accountability placed on educators today and the greater expectation to provide instruction that ensures all students are successful. The increase in alternative certification routes to teaching, increasing standards for teaching and certification, the retirement of the Baby Boomer generation, and the need to attract a more diverse population to teaching are additional reasons for the surge in use of formal mentoring approaches. Informal approaches to mentoring are no longer viewed as sufficient for the needs of today's beginning educators and schools.

Considering these factors, it is no wonder that by 1998 mentoring of beginning teachers was mandated and funded in twenty-nine states in the United States and required in various forms in a number of others (Sweeny 1998). Mentoring is an investment in the success of both beginning teachers and the thousands of students whose lives those teachers will touch throughout their careers. Mentoring also protects that investment by dramatically increasing the retention of beginning teachers, saving organizations the loss of several thousands of dollars when a teacher leaves.

What Is a Mentor?

The fundamental means for providing beginning teacher support is, of course, the mentor. A mentor is a person who assumes the *primary responsibility* to provide mentoring (see Figure 1.1). The mentor is described this way because there are several approaches for providing the assistance, support, and guidance beginning teachers deserve. Each approach incorporates a different conception of mentoring and purposes for induction. At this point, we need to consider the impact of one's concept of a mentor on the choices one makes about structuring the induction and mentoring program.

Defining a Mentor

At the most fundamental level, the mentor is always a role model. No one disagrees with this statement, because everyone who uses a mentoring strategy is interested in novices learning from experts who are the kind of role models leaders want novices to emulate. Where disagreement sometimes occurs is in answering the question, "What is it a mentor should be modeling?"

The earliest mentoring programs used approaches that at least implied that the mentor was an expert with all the answers, whose job was to provide the answers to the novice and to ensure that the novice eventually became someone who had all the answers too. I call that approach to mentoring the mentor cloning model. I know the label exaggerates this position a bit, but I urge leaders to examine their concept of the mentor to be sure it does not look like this exaggerated cloning process. I have observed many mentoring programs with mentors who at least act as if cloning themselves is their purpose.

Today's educators recognize the cloning model of mentoring as less than professional and out of sync with current conceptions of learning and teaching as more of a constructivist process. They know excellence in teaching and excellence in learning to teach is as much an art as it is a science. Thus, I propose that the mentors that educators need today must act more as models of continual learning than as individuals who have all the answers. This is a crucial understanding to reach and to implement in induction and mentoring processes. This conception of teaching and learning cannot be learned by new teachers if they are inducted into the profession any other way.

Simply stated, if mentors act as if they have all the answers and are not continuing to learn, new teachers will learn to look for and act as if they have all the answers, encouraging the idea that they do not need to keep learning once they have found a teaching style that works. Put such a teacher into a classroom and you get students who perceive their roles as getting the right answers, and when they have done that, it is okay to stop learning. This is exactly what educational leaders do not want to see.

What leaders *do* want to see is an aligned three-layer model of continual learning:

1. Leaders want to see mentors who model the excitement of learning every day, openly, and in front of their peers. They want to see mentors with a drive to find ever better ways to help their students *and* their colleagues succeed.
2. With this kind of mentoring, beginning teachers become models of continual learning, and do so openly, in front of their students. Leaders want to see beginning teachers whose passion is finding ever better and more effective ways of ensuring their students' success.
3. Leaders need this kind of beginning teacher, because they know it is the best way to help students become lifelong learners and collaborative workers who are open to learning from each other, always searching for better and more effective ways to achieve their own goals.

Clarifying what mentors should model is an absolutely critical step in developing induction and mentoring programs that can actually improve teaching and increase student success. Leaders who are responsible for the success of induction and mentoring programs and of beginning teachers need to establish this starting point before they make the next set of decisions.

The Evolving Picture of the Protégé

It is becoming quite surprising to review the range and diversity of prior experience found in new employees at a typical start-of-school orientation meeting. Some are twenty-one years old, recently graduated from college, and ready to assume their first paid position in a new career. Some of these individuals have never held a paid position before, not even a part-time job for a few weeks during school breaks. Others may be in their late thirties or older, have raised several children, and are now returning to a career they started fifteen years earlier. Some have been actively teaching for a number of years and are merely changing districts or schools, or even just grade levels. Still others have been working for a number of years in a corporate position or the military, have recently attained a teaching degree and certification, and are changing careers to become teachers. A more recent phenomenon is the new employee who has worked in another career, has no preparation as a teacher, is filling a teaching position in a subject area where candidates are scarce, and is entering this role under an alternative certification program.

Creators of induction and mentoring programs must carefully seek ways to adjust the support provided to such a diverse range of new employees so that the assistance they receive remains appropriate to the varying levels and types of experience new employees bring to their work. It is critical that the program address the individual needs that determine the ability of the person to develop professionally. It is also essential to explicitly model how important it is for all educators to work for the success of individual learners.

Induction and mentoring are frequently tailored to the different levels of new employee experience. Following are three terms induction and mentoring programs often use to distinguish these levels of need and the way the program delivers its services. Those who lead an induction program need to select, define for others, and consistently use a similar set of terms in their work. (See also Figure 1.1)

1. **Protégé:** The labels programs give new participants in mentoring vary considerably, from mentee to partner teacher to colleague. I use the term *protégé* and reserve it exclusively for those new or beginning educators who are assigned to and actively work with a mentor. This is to distinguish the protégé from all other new employees, regardless of their level of experience, who are not working with mentors.

2. **Beginning educator:** This term includes both teachers and others such as school social workers, school psychologists, school nurses, or learning center directors. *Beginning educator* usually describes someone with little or no previous professional educational experience, such as those with a year or less of teaching experience. The label *beginner* also assumes no previous experience. In other words, someone who taught for four years, then raised a family, and is now returning to teaching should *not* be called a beginning educator, even if the lack of recent experience suggests a need for intensive mentoring.

A mentor assigned to a beginning educator needs to be cautious, for the protégé frequently has other kinds of experience that greatly impact his or her professional development needs. For example, mentors should not treat a twenty-one-year-old college graduate the same way they would a thirty-five-year-old individual who has entered the profession through an alternative route to teaching after working in a related content field, or the same way as a forty-two-year-old beginning educator who has just raised two children, and has recently completed requirements for a teaching certificate. Both the individuals mentioned in the last two circumstances represent people who have life experiences that have prepared them well for many aspects of the role of educator, even though they may have little or no paid educational experience. Nevertheless, in all three cases the term *beginning educator* applies.

How does mentoring of a beginner get started? Beginning educators may not know all the questions they need to ask, and so they may feel well prepared and ready to go to work when, in fact, they are not well prepared. Mentors should expect that beginning educators may not always be ready to accept help immediately, but that they may become ready and more open to help a little later in their teaching experience. During that time mentors must remain visibly and continually available and accepting of the level of readiness their protégé expresses. The experience of organizing and running one's own classroom and the sense of responsibility for student success is a huge reality check for many beginning teachers. This is why they may have an intense and sudden need for mentoring once the first days or weeks of the school year are past.

Mentors need to stay on top of their own responsibilities, trying to accomplish their own work well in advance of when things usually have to be done. This is important because when the beginning teacher grasps the reality of teaching and becomes aware of his or her need for help, the mentor must have time to provide the necessary support. For example, if a mentor waits to complete her own grading until just before report cards are due, she will not be available to help her protégé with that task when the need arises. In this case, the opportunity to explain issues of student assessment and fairness, discuss district assessment expectations and processes, and demonstrate important decision-making processes are lost. Or, the mentor may make time to help the protégé, but may end up with insufficient time to do justice to his or her own grading.

3. **New educator:** This term refers to educators who are newly hired to the district, but have at least two years of paid professional teaching experience. They may have been recently employed as educators in another district or may be returning to education after an extended leave, but they have nearly similar needs for orientation to the school, district, community, curriculum, key people, procedures, and the traditions and culture of the school. However, they do not always need the same amount of time and the same intensity of mentoring to become well oriented to these things. That is why it is critical to distinguish between beginning and new educators.

Structures for Induction and Mentoring Programs

Experienced but new educators know most of the questions that should be asked and are usually not timid about asking those questions or seeking the assistance they know they need. As a result, they can anticipate many of their needs and can learn the ropes much faster. Mentors assigned to an experienced educator may find their protégé provides as much leadership in the relationship and in accomplishing tasks as they do. Mentors who know this pattern may occur will view it as a good sign. They will be comfortable when this occurs, knowing that the new educator's needs are being met one way or the other and that their protégé is developing appropriately.

Mentors who are not well prepared to do mentoring may feel disappointed that they cannot help this kind of protégé more, and may be defensive and insistent about who should be leading in the mentoring relationship. Such a reaction is unfortunate and should be avoided. A strong mentor training program, a focus on meeting the varying needs of the protégés, and a mentoring process that predicts the phases through which new employees will move all help mentors to anticipate what they need to do to remain appropriate in their mentoring and to facilitate their protégés' professional growth.

Administrators and educational leaders who want their induction and mentoring programs to have a major positive impact on the success of their new employees need to ensure that their program components are structured to take into account the diversity of protégés' experience. Orientation seminars, for example, can begin with whole group activities, but should be customized to grade or course level for introductions to curriculum and strategies that are specific to particular levels of instruction. The support should also be individualized, although it does not necessarily have to be delivered individually. Mentoring is provided precisely to ensure that the critical knowledge gained in group settings is individualized to the needs of the educator, successfully mastered, and applied in every teacher's classroom.

SkyLight Professional Development

Individual or Team Mentoring?

Even though most programs adopt the traditional one-to-one mentoring relationship for their program's approach, some may question whether that is the best structure. Other possibilities exist, which is why the mentor was defined earlier as the person who assumes the primary responsibility to provide mentoring. Individual, one-on-one mentoring is the prevalent structure because it is the easiest way to resolve a number of issues. Reducing mentoring to a pair context makes it easier to create the safe, confidential, and trusting relationship that must be present if mentoring is to successfully prompt the risk-taking and professional growth needed. Also, one-to-one mentoring simplifies assigning the responsibilities necessary in a mentoring relationship, simplifies the training and support needed by mentors, and is the most practical structure for mentoring in many schools, especially those with only a few teachers in any given grade or department. However, other approaches can be successfully used.

The use of a team approach to mentoring is increasing, especially as program leaders decide they want to develop beginning teachers who see teaching as a team function, not just as an isolated, individual role. Schools that are consciously trying to help all students succeed often structure the staff in teams so that the diverse strengths of team members can be better used to address the diverse needs of students. This conception of teaching suggests that mentoring should also be a model of team collaboration so that it reinforces other efforts to develop beginning teachers for the team environment. In such a context, group or team mentoring makes a great deal of sense, even though there are several challenges to implementing the strategy effectively and efficiently. Leaders can help make the process go smoothly by providing the time and facilitating the conversation needed to coordinate a team's responsibilities for mentoring. Providing training for a team of people is more difficult to coordinate and may be more costly. However, the effort is worth it as it increases the number of experienced teachers involved in mentoring. This helps a school to create an experienced faculty with the very skills excellent teachers need. After all, mentoring strategies and skills are also critical for good teaching.

Even in a team mentoring situation, however, one person should be identified as responsible for making sure the protégé is effectively supported. This is necessary regardless of whether the mentor or other team members are actually the individuals who provide the specific assistance that is needed. In this way, the person who is assigned the oversight responsibility often acts more as a linking agent between the protégé and the team, helping the protégé assess his or her own needs and access the people and resources available from the team.

There is another reason to consider the use of team mentoring. Almost all induction and mentoring programs are based on the idea that separation of mentoring from summative evaluation is required to ensure that the environment in the mentoring relationship is conducive to candid self-assessment, risk-taking, learning, and professional growth. In some novice teacher support programs, however, tricky roles and tasks must be assigned. For example, some state-mandated programs require evaluation of the beginning teacher for purposes of earning a professional certificate. In these types of situations, team mentoring can be used to separate the assigned responsibilities so that a principal on the support team does the observation and conferences for purposes of evaluation, contract extension, and certification, and mentors observe and confer with the protégé for purposes of supporting improvement in performance. Such a delineation of roles recognizes that principals do play critical mentoring roles, but also acknowledges that novice teachers are not likely to seek help from an evaluator, and thus mentoring should be kept separate from evaluation.

Full-Time or Part-Time Mentoring?

The most common mentoring structure is a teacher with a full-time teaching responsibility assigned to also serve as a mentor for a beginning teacher. In this case, the mentoring pair must find the time to plan, problem solve, observe, discuss teaching, set goals, and so forth (Moller 1999). This approach to mentoring is frequently accompanied by a stipend for the mentor in recognition of the tremendous amount of extra time it takes to be an effective mentor. For example, it is often necessary for mentors to use their own planning periods to assist their protégés. Providing a stipend is recognition that a mentor teacher's own work of calling parents, developing materials, or conducting planning must be done outside of the school day on his or her own time. In some situations, leaders of induction programs may not have the resources or may not wish to provide a mentoring stipend, but they also know there is a need for time for mentoring, particularly if instructional improvement is a program purpose. In that case, the mentoring pair is often provided with a budget of substitute time on which to draw throughout the year whenever planning time, staff development, observations, or coaching conferences are needed in the mentoring process.

In smaller schools and school districts, providing substitute teachers is often the most practical way to create the time needed for effective mentoring. However, finding substitutes at certain times of the year is difficult and results in the best teachers being sometimes absent from their own classrooms. While it is fairly logical to justify the sacrifice made today on behalf of the students who will benefit throughout the protégé's entire career, the arrangement does cause breaks in instructional consistency and other problems. The fact is, at least using this approach, the time for mentoring must be taken from time in the mentor's own classroom (Moller 1999), or the additional time must be purchased, either through a stipend or extended contract and school year.

A different approach makes finding time for professional development a greater priority. This approach is generally described as restructuring, and it often requires a complete analysis of how time is currently spent compared to the needs for professional development and school improvement on a daily basis during the school day. This step is frequently taken when district or school administrators realize they must align the use of time to their expectations that teachers improve their professional practice. Simply put, they decide they must provide the tools for people to do the work that is expected. Barkley (1999) reflects this approach and provides some powerful means for resolving the issue of making time available for initiatives such as mentoring and coaching. I have found the following strategies to be helpful in resolving time issues:

- Release mentors from hallway and/or study hall supervision or other non-instructional duties.
- Allow for team teaching between two mentors, or a mentor and a protégé.
- Use technology, mathematics/science, or literacy staff development funds to provide a year or two release for a teacher to serve as a mentor to beginning teachers and to experienced teachers in the target staff development program.

The Benefits of Full-Time Mentoring

Some larger mentoring programs have concluded they have a sufficient number of novice teachers to assign a full-time mentor to a number of protégés for a period of two to three years. Such a configuration is much more common today, and is used in cities such as Milwaukee, Minneapolis, and Baltimore, and in some suburban systems such as Cherry Creek Schools in Colorado (Romer 1999). In these situations, mentors are released from all teaching responsibilities, replaced by another teacher, and assigned to work intensely with as few as five or as many as twelve to fifteen protégés at a time. This range results from the different kinds of expectations placed on the mentor for improving instruction and other goals. Generally, the more complex the assignment, the more time needed with each protégé to attain the desired results within the formal mentoring period.

Despite the cost of additional salaries, these districts find a sufficient return on their investment to warrant the use of this approach. Consider what Terri Romer, a full-time mentor in Colorado's Cherry Creek Schools S.T.A.R. (Staff Training Assistance and Review) Mentor Program has to say about full-time mentoring:

I think that one tremendous plus in being a full-time mentor is not having the responsibilities of a classroom full of children and being able to concentrate solely on the needs and growth of our mentees.

We were told recently by a secondary administrator that the first year teachers in his school who have had a S.T.A.R. mentor have grown at a pace that equals three or more years of a new teacher without a mentor. This fantastic growth is due to three facts:

1. Full-time mentors can exclusively devote their time to assisting, advising, and coaching the mentees to cause that growth!

2. Full-time mentors can spend in-depth, extended time with their mentees as needed. No other commitments get in the way. As a result, we get to know our mentees so quickly and "intimately" that individual needs, worries, plans, idiosyncrasies, strengths, etc., can really be discovered and acted on. I truly know each mentee so well as an individual that I am able to be a better mentor.

3. The third reason we are so successful is what we call our data curtain. What we mean is that, in our program, there is an imaginary wall around the mentoring relationship. Nothing discussed within the mentoring pair can ever be shared outside that relationship. We have found that this data curtain protects the confidentiality of the mentoring dialogue and ensures that the mentee will feel free to discuss their real problems and concerns with me. Then we go to work on whatever it is. Of course, this is something part-time mentors should do too.

With this kind of closeness and time, great strides can quickly be made in developing trust and achieving candid and open communication with every mentee. That is why full-time mentoring increases the opportunity for growth and mentee improvement accelerates so much. Other mentoring programs should consider the use of full-time mentors too.

(Romer 1999)

Structures for Induction and Mentoring Programs

Every educator knows the terrible tensions created by the scarcity of time in schools. The Cherry Creek S.T.A.R. Mentor Program and others like it around the country have learned how to avoid that problem while better supporting their beginning teachers. These programs are achieving outstanding results. The return on investment they have found also comes from cost and other savings, including the following:

- Eliminated costs of mentoring stipends
- Decreased problems with finding and frequency for using substitute teachers
- Decreased costs for substitute teachers
- Eliminated disruptions to instruction in the mentor's classroom
- Accelerated professional growth for both the mentor and protégé
- Decreased costs for recruitment, orientation, and training of new teachers because of increased retention of teachers
- Decreased waste of administrative time because of increased teacher retention
- Decrease in the administrative time required to supervise and evaluate new teachers since their performance is better because of their work with their mentor

Full-time assignment of a mentor is effective, because it restructures the use of time and aligns it with the priority of improving instruction in the protégé's classroom. Such dedicated time clarifies for all staff the district's commitment to the innovative practices that time supports (Hayes et al. 1999). Furthermore, full-time mentoring eliminates the inherent conflict between the need of the students in the protégé's classroom for a quality teacher and the need of the students in the mentor's own classroom for a quality teacher. When that conflict is left unresolved or is even increased by placing excessive expectations on part-time mentors, the students in the mentor's classroom will win, and the mentoring process and the students in the protégé's classroom will lose. This conflict is really a lose-lose situation, because it is always unfair to someone (Moller 1999).

While the full-time assignment of mentors is not a configuration that is appropriate for every mentoring program, it is a win-win situation many programs should consider. It is a solution to a number of the problems that occur when the mentoring role is added on top of everything else a mentor is already doing as a full-time teacher.

Critical Distinctions That Make All the Difference

One concern of educational leaders involves the interaction of mentors with nonparticipant colleagues within the traditional egalitarian culture of schools. In this culture, all teachers are perceived as the same except for differences in teaching style. Leaders often want to avoid the "sibling rivalry" and resulting ostracism that can occur when teachers are singled out as unique (Magee 1999). However, leaders also want to establish a culture of shared leadership in which teachers can offer themselves as resources for professional responsibilities that go beyond teaching, such as mentoring (Gusky and Peterson 1996). Of course, leaders know there are often enormous differences in the effectiveness of some teachers, in teachers' people skills, in their willingness to help others, and so forth. These are the very things leaders consider when selecting and matching mentors to novice teachers. Effective leaders match the needs of a beginner to the strengths of a mentor and expect that considerable transfer of experience and professional learning will occur. For example, a principal may hire a beginning teacher with excellent credentials, but no previous experience and few technology skills. To increase the opportunity for this teacher's success, the mentor should have considerable experience—especially in using technology in the curriculum. Leaders know the difference between the partners will challenge assumptions, lead to discoveries, and prompt the professional growth all beginning teachers need. Without the difference between mentor and protégé, beginning teachers' assumptions about the ability of all students to learn, the role of the teacher, and even the career of teaching may remain those that they formed during their previous years as students. These assumptions are often inadequate when applied to today's schools and students.

The mentor is able to function as a mentor precisely because of greater experience and knowledge, deeper insights into student learning, and greater skills at facilitating that learning. The differences between the mentor and the protégé make the mentoring worthwhile for the beginning educator. Protégés stand to gain more from working with someone who is different from them than from someone whose experiences and perspectives are similar to their own. By design, therefore, effective mentoring cannot be a peer relationship.

Nevertheless, the traditional school culture reinforces peer relationships, and this can make mentors uncomfortable if they feel singled out for different status and use of time than their colleagues (Moller 1999). This dilemma must be explicitly addressed in program design and during mentor training so that mentors are prepared to deal with it positively (Bird 1986). People who are not participating in a mentoring program may be uncomfortable with teacher leadership, and these colleagues may make comments that reflect that discomfort. Teaching mentors to respond positively to the discomfort can ultimately save a mentoring program from becoming a very limited orientation program in which the mentor's role in facilitating professional growth is too frightening for some to undertake.

Dealing with Distinctions

Clarity about vocabulary can be a helpful starting point for dealing with these tricky distinctions. For example, when coaching occurs within a mentoring relationship, I suggest that it not be called peer coaching. Such a label seems imprecise in that while the job description (teacher) may be the same, there are a number of significant differences between the beginning and the experienced teachers in the mentoring pair. I suggest that the term *peer coaching* be reserved to describe the coaching that occurs between two or more veteran educators who may have differing strengths but whose years of experience are more similar.

Those who choose to label mentoring as peer mentoring or a mentor's coaching as peer coaching are usually trying to distinguish it from the mentoring and coaching done by a supervisor or administrator who is also an evaluator of the beginning teacher. I suggest that leaders find other, more helpful ways to make these vital distinctions, such as differentiating between the process and purposes of coaching and evaluation. Figure 1.3 offers guidance regarding how leaders can do this.

Use of the term *peer* in the mentoring context is also a reaction to the discomfort described earlier. Traditionally, teachers have tried not to call attention to the ways in which they are different from each other. Such an approach is understandable but often unfortunate, for it limits the opportunities for learning from each other. The use of mentoring raises issues of teacher leadership because leadership is what the role of the mentor requires. In fact, establishing teacher leadership as a norm is one of the biggest benefits of mentoring. As important as this is for school improvement, it is still a big change for many teachers, and leaders need to know how to successfully facilitate that transition.

Clarifying the Critical Differences in Roles

Features	Mentor Coaching	Peer Coaching	Supervisory Evaluation
The Focus of the Observation	Set by the interests and needs of the teacher to be observed, often after observation of an effective teacher that prompts discovery of a need to improve	A mutual inquiry into increased use of the best instructional practices in both parties' teaching	Comparison of the teacher's skills with a model of excellent teaching or a set of teaching standards to determine minimal competency
The Direction of the Focus	Protégé ⇄ Mentor	Best Practices → Teacher A Teacher B	Teacher ← Evaluator
The Goals of the Activity	• To develop a more trusting and collegial professional relationship • To develop reflective, analytical and self-assessment skills in protégés and mentors • To develop more effective teaching strategies • To improve student learning	• To develop a more trusting and collegial professional relationship • To develop reflective, analytical, and self-assessment skills of both • To develop more effective teaching strategies for both • To improve student learning in both classrooms	• To judge teacher competence for decisions about certification and continued employment • To apply pressure to increase teacher performance and accountability • To improve student learning
Observation Initiated By	Mentor, first by invitation to the protégé to observe the mentor at work. Then, after comfort is established, mentor observation in the protégé's classroom	Either teacher in the peer coaching pair	The supervising administrator in response to legal and contractual requirements
The Paper Trail and Use of the Observational Data	• Copies kept by both • Both look for data patterns. • Mentor asks protégé reflective questions to teach him or her how to self-assess and reflect	• Given to the teacher who was observed to analyze • Coach asks reflective questions to prompt teacher's analysis	• Evaluator analyzes the data and prescribes needed improvement • Papers go into personnel file as documentation of evaluation

Figure 1.3

SkyLight Professional Development

REFERENCES

Barkley, S. G. 1999. Time: It's made, not found. *Journal of Staff Development*. 20(4): 37–39.

Bird, T. 1986. *The mentor's dilemma.* San Francisco: Far West Regional Educational Laboratory.

Gusky, T., and K. D. Peterson. 1996. The road to classroom change. *Educational Leadership*. 53(4): 10–14.

Hayes, C., P. Grippe, and G. Hall. 1999. Firmly planted. *Journal of Staff Development*. 20(4): 17–21.

Magee, M. 1999. The curse of the trophy. *Journal of Staff Development*. 10(4): 23–26.

Moller, G. 1999. At issue: Teacher leadership. *Journal of Staff Development*. 20(4): 11–15.

Romer, T. 1999, November. An e-mail message to Barry Sweeney regarding the benefits and results of full-time mentoring.

Sweeney, B. W. 1994. *Promoting the growth of new teachers: A mentor training manual.* Wheaton, IL: Resources for Staff and Organization Development.

———. 1998. *A survey of state-mandated mentoring and new teacher induction programs in the 50 United States.* Wheaton, IL: Best Practice Resources. Online at <www.teachermentors.com/MCenter%20Site/StateList.html>.

Two Blackline masters are provided on the pages that follow:
- Suggested Mentor Activities Before Starting School
- Suggested Mentor Activities During First and Second Weeks

Both offer ideas for mentors in the beginning of the induction and mentoring process. Once mentors understand the terms and basic structure of the mentoring process, as described in this selection, they may use these lists to jump start the induction and mentoring program.

Suggested Mentor Activities Before Starting School

Not every task on this list makes sense for every teacher when they first begin teaching. Identify appropriate activities given the experience of your protégé, and then check off tasks as you complete them.

BUILDING TOUR:

School layout and location of:

- ❑ Washrooms
- ❑ Lounge
- ❑ Office
- ❑ Supply room
- ❑ Custodian
- ❑ Media center and audiovisual equipment
- ❑ Bus entrance and teacher parking
- ❑ Rooms for specialists, nurse, social worker, psychologist, music/art/physical education

TOUR OF OTHER IMPORTANT PLACES:

- ❑ The school service center (administration building)
- ❑ Location and time of first day Institute activities (map?)
- ❑ The teacher center (and their hours and services)
- ❑ Local "teacher store"
- ❑ Good lunch spots

BUILDING PROCEDURES:

- ❑ Hours for teachers, building use at other times
- ❑ Extra duties, bus, clubs, activities, chaperoning
- ❑ Attendance policies
- ❑ Movement of children, entry/exit from building, washrooms, lunch
- ❑ Student and teacher dress code
- ❑ Fire/disaster drills
- ❑ Lunch supervision, eating arrangements
- ❑ Homework, testing policies
- ❑ Student accidents, emergencies
- ❑ Pullout programs and the need for flexibility

(continued on next page)

ACCESS TO RESOURCES:

- ❏ Classroom and teaching supply requisitions, budget process
- ❏ Audiovisual equipment requests
- ❏ Computer access for teacher use and for student use
- ❏ Discretionary funds (saving receipts)
- ❏ Shared equipment and materials
- ❏ Textbooks, supplemental materials

STUDENT DISCIPLINE:

- ❏ Behavior expectations for hallway, lunch, washroom, playground
- ❏ Establishing and enforcing classroom behavior expectations and routines
- ❏ What works for me with our children
- ❏ Consequences for extreme behavior problems (contact parent, referral)
- ❏ Expected staff supervision outside of classroom
- ❏ Referral process for students with special needs (gifted, special education)

CURRICULUM:

- ❏ Guides/manuals
- ❏ District curriculum development process and resulting expectations for teachers
- ❏ Central office staff in curriculum and staff development (Department of Instruction)
- ❏ Management of the curriculum demands and pacing of learning
- ❏ Introduction to texts and available supplemental materials
- ❏ Lesson plan procedures and expectations
- ❏ Classroom assessment system, rubrics, and tests as feedback for instruction
- ❏ Subject matter experts on the building staff
- ❏ Teaching teams or shared responsibilities
- ❏ Grading procedures for day-to-day records (report cards later)
- ❏ Opening day schedule, appropriate plans, administrative details
- ❏ A plan for the first week's lessons (allow for organizing and behavioral teaching)
- ❏ Curriculum mapping (scope and sequence)

(continued on next page)

Blackline 1.1 (continued)

ACCOUNTABILITY FOR STUDENT LEARNING:

- ❏ District strategic planning process and objective, and implications for teaching
- ❏ School improvement planning process, implications of the plan for grade/department level decisions, and individual teaching practices
- ❏ Student learning standards and district curriculum goals and expectations for teaching
- ❏ State assessment schedules, and process and preparation approach (overview only)
- ❏ District assessment system, rubrics, standardized test schedules

ORGANIZING THE CLASSROOM:

- ❏ Options for room arrangement and effect on teaching and learning
- ❏ Traffic patterns
- ❏ Student work collection and distribution system
- ❏ Storage and access to materials
- ❏ Student access to texts, equipment, and teaching centers

PERSONAL AND PROFESSIONAL DECISIONS AND PROCEDURES:

- ❏ Calling in sick and personal or professional days
- ❏ Expectations for sharing with colleagues, what others can do for you
- ❏ Adjustment to a new job
- ❏ Performance review (evaluation)
- ❏ Professional portfolios

Blackline 1.1 (continued)

Suggested Mentor Activities During First and Second Weeks

Not every task on this list makes sense for every teacher, but many will be important to do soon after your protégé arrives at your school. Identify which of these activities are appropriate for your school and for your protégé, then check off those tasks as you complete them.

HOW IS IT GOING?
- ❏ Don't wait—ask about concerns, new ideas, or proud moments.
- ❏ Share your experiences too. (We all work at these same issues.)
- ❏ How can I help? *I'm available at . . .* , or *Let's work together on . . . .*
- ❏ Provide encouragement, show enthusiasm for successes, and look for ways to celebrate.
- ❏ Only provide feedback or other options when requested or when the answer is clearly one "right way."
- ❏ Give protégés the okay to blow the whistle when they are about to overload on too much information or extra time.

BUILDING AND DISTRICT REQUIREMENTS:
- ❏ Sub folder, lesson plans, requests for specific substitutes
- ❏ Faculty members, timing, and schedule for team meetings, etc.
- ❏ School calendar for the year including end of quarter, holidays, and assemblies
- ❏ Progress report procedures
- ❏ Report card processes and deadlines
- ❏ Professional staff evaluation process
- ❏ Contractual requirements for non-tenured staff such as workshops or visits

HELPING CHILDREN WITH SPECIAL NEEDS:
- ❏ Staffing or placement procedures
- ❏ Cumulative records and the issue of confidentiality
- ❏ Avoid compromising situations when trying to help, such as offering rides, etc.
- ❏ Introductions to support staff, gifted, reading, LAP, LD/BD, speech, social worker, psychologist, nurse, guidance, etc.

PERSONAL AND PROFESSIONAL TOPICS:
- ❏ Opportunities for attendance at professional meetings/workshops
- ❏ Importance of attending meetings that explain expectations and changes
- ❏ Get the new teacher and a few colleagues away from the building for a social gathering to begin friendships.
- ❏ Explain mentor's class schedule and availability. Are calls at mentor's home OK?

Blackline 1.2

Mentors provide a mirror to help new teachers get an accurate image of their classroom. Pitton suggests strategies to help mentees reflect on their teaching and make adjustments to meet the diverse needs of their students.

Addressing the Needs of the Mentee

by **Debra Pitton**

The Need to Accurately See What Is Happening in the Classroom

In the early stages of teaching, many mentees are unable to see the big picture. They are often unaware of how (or if) students are learning and may not notice much of what is going on in their classrooms because they are so focused on their own actions as the teacher. This limited vision inhibits their ability to reflect on interactions that create positive learning experiences. During the early stages, when mentees are learning how to become comfortable with the role of teacher, mentors need to reflect back to mentees what they see during their observations. Providing a description of what is going on during a lesson without qualifying it (i.e., that was right, that was wrong) is important.

Initially, mentors must provide mentees with a "mirror" to allow them to get an accurate image of their classrooms. A video camera provides an exact image, but sometimes when viewing a tape mentees can only see themselves and their own actions, as opposed to student response or interactions with students. In addition, new teachers may

Adapted from *Mentoring Novice Teachers* by D. Pitton, pp. 41–50. © 2000 by SkyLight Training and Publishing.

feel overwhelmed after viewing all the things happening in the classroom that are caught on tape. A more comfortable way of providing a mirror is for the mentor to reiterate what happened in the classroom. Accurate descriptions of the events, conversations, and behaviors observed in a classroom, without judgment or praise, are a powerful support for a mentee's learning. New teachers may not be aware of all that is going on in their classrooms. A written description lets them "see" their classroom interactions more closely. Initial, informal conversations about observations are a good starting point. The following dialogue gives mentors practice presenting neutral classroom observations to their mentees.

Scenario: Mirroring a Classroom

Review the following scenario, or role-play it with a colleague. When you are finished, use the questions following the role-play to give another mentor or a colleague a description of what you saw in a nonjudgmental way. If you are working alone, write down your thoughts or use a tape recorder to capture your comments. Reread or listen to them after you have completed the task. Work to mirror what you saw and avoid making any qualifying remarks.

SETTING: An 8th grade middle school language arts classroom is asked to get into groups for a brainstorming session.

TEACHER: Okay, kids, we finished reading *The Outsiders* yesterday, so now I want you to get into groups and brainstorm ideas so you can write an essay on the theme. So why don't you find three other people and get into your groups. (*Students begin pulling chairs across the room and calling out to friends to form groups. Some sit alone and look around. The teacher picks up a stack of papers.*)

TEACHER: While you are getting yourselves together, I will hand out the form I want you to complete as you brainstorm. It's really easy, but all of you need to contribute to the group to get it done. Okay, okay, get in your groups now. Somebody needs to get together with Sammy, he's all by himself over there. (*Teacher walks to the still-forming groups and hands out a form to every student.*)

STUDENT: Do we all need to fill this out?

TEACHER: Yes, but you need to work together. (*To the class*) You will all need a brainstorming sheet to do the essay. Hey, quiet down—you're not babies and you should be able to get into groups without so much noise, for crying out loud! (*Students finalize their groups and Sammy pulls his desk to the side of a group of three other students. A student raises her hand.*)

TEACHER: Yes, Shondra?

SHONDRA: I don't get what you mean by brainstorming.

TEACHER: It's just a list of ideas that could be the focus of your writing. You have to have a thesis, you know, and this is a way to capture all of your ideas so you can narrow down your choices and determine the one that you want to write about. Remember that theme is what the author is trying to tell us in the book, the message. This form gives you a list of the characters and key events in the book to use as a springboard for your ideas—so get busy.

Dialogue: Observation

What did you hear in the scenario you read or heard? How would you mirror this teaching event back to the teacher without qualifying what occurred? Answer the following questions to practice reflecting back events.

When watching your class I saw . . .
When observing your class I heard . . .

Now share your comments with a colleague and discuss the differences between your statements.

Feedback to the previous scenario such as "You should have explained brainstorming before passing out the assignment," "This would work better," or "I always do it this way" does not allow novice teachers to see what is happening in the classroom. These types of comments indicate that a mentor is doing more than just mirroring what happened. Mentors also should be careful not to overwhelm their mentee by listing every area of concern from an observation. Mentors should select one particular area, such as the teacher's use of language in the dialogue above, and reflect back the actual statements used by the teacher. For example, the mentor might say, "I heard you say to the students that what they were going to do was easy, and another time you told them that they were not babies and should be able to get into groups without so much noise." The mentee may respond with an explanation of why something happened or an idea about what he or she might need to do in the future. However, in the initial stages of teacher development mentors may need to be more directive to get mentees to reflect. Following up a reflected statement such as the one in the example above with a question such as "What do you think about that?" enables mentors to avoid making judgments about what they heard and prompts mentees to reflect. If mentees do not recognize areas where they need to be more direct, mentors need to use "I" messages. "I noticed that Carlie was drawing pictures during your explanation, and I wonder what you might do to address this" is an example of a direct statement that is not accusatory because it focuses on the observer's perspective. Even with direct statements, mentors need to use language that will not create defensiveness on the part of the mentee, and "I" messages can help.

Once mentees have reflected on their areas of development, mentors need to offer them some resources. In the situation outlined above, recommending a book about communication in the classroom or suggesting that the novice teacher visit a teacher who is savvy in classroom communications provides the novice with a way to gather information. Finally, mentors need to ask mentees what their plans are for addressing the issue. Accessing the resources is the first step, but mentees also need to identify specific steps they will take to improve in the area of concern. This process should be used on one or two concerns at a time. When mentors mirror all the negative things they see in their mentees' classrooms, their mentees can become overwhelmed, rendering the mirroring ineffective.

Mentors also need to mirror the positive things they see. For example, a positive reflection mentors could share from the scenario above is "I saw that you were using cooperative learning and had structured the activity with a form for the students to use." All reflections of classroom activity need to include images of strength as well as areas of concern. Novice teachers cannot tackle four or five separate issues at a time. Mentors should focus on the most obvious or crucial issues, and then balance the reflection by identifying what went well in the lesson.

Mentors may use the Observation Note Form in Figure 2.1 as a tool to gather information during early observations. This form provides mentors with statements they can make and questions they can ask to foster reflection following an observation.

The Need for Guiding Questions

After mentors provide mentees with a description of what is happening in the classroom, it is hoped that they will recognize the need for some action or change. At this point mentees may specifically ask for help and guidance. Observations and questions that indicate that a mentee is aware that he or she must shift the focus to the students include "I could see that some of the students really didn't get it," "They really weren't listening to me, were they?" "How do I get them to listen to me?" and "How can I increase their ability to stay on task?" If mentees do not identify issues to address from the classroom reflection, mentors can ask guiding questions to help them consider the classroom interactions more thoughtfully. Questions that can help probe the mentee's awareness include "Why do you think this happened?", "What was your goal at this point?", and "What might have caused the students to respond that way?" The focus of questions is not about telling mentees what to do, but rather about helping them discover ways to improve their teaching and supporting their efforts to learn and grow. Although some mentees quickly move beyond the self-centered stage and begin to focus on their students, mentors need to continue to observe and reflect what they see to their mentees to support their growth.

If questions do not help to prompt a novice teacher's awareness of areas for growth, mentors must be more directive. One way to do this is to role-play. By asking mentees to role-play the student (or parent, administrator, or whoever), mentors can

Observation Note Form

Complete the mentor portion of the form, then share it with your mentee. Ask your mentee the designated questions, fill in the mentee's comments, and then ask the mentee what steps can be taken to address areas of concern and maintain positive areas.

Observation Notes

Mentor:_____   Date: _____

Mentee:_____   Class/grade: _____

When watching your class I saw . . .
(List one positive observation.)

What do you think about that?
(Fill in mentee response.)

When watching your class I saw . . .
(List one area of concern from the observation.)

What do you think about that?
(Fill in mentee response.)

When observing your class I heard . . .
(List one positive statement you heard.)

What do you think about that?
(Fill in mentee response.)

When observing your class I heard . . .
(List one statement you heard that might be a concern.)

What do you think about that?
(Fill in mentee response.)

Next Steps:

Figure 2.1

role-play how mentees might respond to a situation more effectively. For example, mentors can set up the role-play by asking the mentee to be the student or parent who was part of a problem. The mentee recreates the comments or actions that precipitated the incident or actions being discussed, and the mentor then role-plays the teacher and provides a response to the situation that reflects a more experienced and/or appropriate perspective.

This type of role-play provides mentees with examples of how they might change their behaviors to match the responses modeled by their mentors. It is a very direct way to give mentees guidance about how they should respond in a given situation. Debriefing after the role-play is important, as this asks mentees to identify what the mentor did that created a more positive outcome. By naming the mentors' behaviors as observed in the role-play, mentees identify specific behaviors they should be using. Another option is for a mentee to role-play him or herself in a situation where the mentor's role is an angry parent or disruptive student (or whatever the area of concern may be) so the mentee can practice what he or she might say and do before facing the real situation. These opportunities are valuable and powerful learning tools.

Mentors can reflect on the following scenario in which a mentor is taking part in a classroom observation to practice asking guiding questions.

Scenario: Observation and Guiding Questions

Read this description of a lesson or have two colleagues role-play it. Look for areas upon which you think this novice teacher can focus her growth.

SETTING: Mary is teaching a track unit to her high school physical education class.

MARY: Okay, we are going to learn about how to do the high jump today.

STUDENT: Who cares about this stuff?

Addressing the Needs of the Mentee

MARY:	If you want to go out for track or watch a friend at a track meet, you need to understand how to successfully complete the high jump. I only have one high jump station, so this half of the class can do stretching exercises from our fitness plans while this half does the jump. (*Mary divides the class, puts half of the students behind her, and tells them to practice stretches.*)
MARY:	(*To the group at the bar*) So your approach is at an angle, see, and you run up to the bar slowly. This isn't about speed, but energy. As you approach, you want to give a kick up, like you would kick a soccer ball, then arch backwards over the pole. (*She demonstrates.*) We will start with the pole low, and see how far you can get.
STUDENT:	I can't do that!
MARY:	Sure you can. (*She lines up the other students and has them practice the jump, raising the bar each time.*)
MARY:	Good job! You should go out for track, Thomas! Why don't you watch Thomas do the jump? Okay. (*Students in the jumping group watch Thomas jump, as do the other group. The stretching group sits around and talks about the weekend and plans for social activities. Mary gives feedback to each student after they jump and helps them improve their approach, takeoff, and jump.*)
MARY:	Okay, you each have gotten to jump several times, let's raise the bar now and see who can keep jumping as it gets higher. Tomorrow (*speaking to the other group*) you guys can go and this group will do the stretches.

Dialogue: Reflecting on Guiding Questions

Review the scenario above using the Observation Note Form (see Figure 2.1). Identify other things you heard or saw in the lesson. After you identify what you heard or saw, determine what types of questions you would ask your mentee to guide him or her to an awareness of what was going on in the class. Write down your thoughts to reflect on later or talk with another mentor to see if you have similar thoughts and ideas.

Scenario: Feedback Conversation

Now read or role-play the actual dialogue that occurred during the feedback conversation for the class described above. This conversation demonstrates the type of guiding questions a mentor might ask after observing this scenario.

MENTOR: Mary, all the students in the second group were able to complete the jump as you demonstrated—that was impressive for their first time.

MARY: Yeah, I think my demonstration was pretty good. I had to practice it a lot because I never did track myself.

MENTOR: I noticed that you divided the class into two groups—can you tell me about that?

MARY: Well, we were supposed to go outside where there are two stations for high jumping. I had planned to have both groups jumping at the same time. But it was raining, so we had to make do with the one station here in the gym. I wanted to do two groups at the same time, but this way I was able to really watch the one group and I gave them pretty specific feedback. I think I was able to note their errors and correct them pretty well. Like you said, all of them got over the bar at least once.

MENTOR: What about the other group?

MARY: Yeah, well, they were working on their stretches, which is part of our ongoing fitness plan.

MENTOR: How successful was this group in getting the stretching done?

MARY: Well, they seemed to be doing their stretches. I mean I know they would have rather been jumping too, but that just wasn't possible. Tomorrow they'll get their turn.

MENTOR: Is there any other way you could organize the jumping with one station so that two groups could go?

MARY: Well, I suppose I could. It just seemed like there would be so many students all waiting in line, and I thought they might not listen to me with everybody talking and stuff.

MENTOR: Do you ever have two groups do an activity and alternate—with one person from each group?

MARY: Oh, yeah, I've done that with some games I've set up. I see how that would work—I didn't think about two groups because I had planned for one so I just went ahead with things basically the same way.

MENTOR: How would it have worked if you had alternated with two groups?

MARY: I guess that would have kept them all involved more, and I could have given the demonstration to all of the students—now I will have to repeat the entire lesson for the second group tomorrow. I think that the group that was supposed to be stretching was not really doing the stretches, so if I had two groups and had them do the stretches while they were waiting their turn, at least they'd all be in front of me so I could see them.

MENTOR: I agree, those ideas would really strengthen your lesson. What will you do now?

MARY: Well, I guess I should give the second group their time to do the jump. But I will at least have the stretching group over in front of me so that I can watch them tomorrow. The next time we do something in groups, I will have to figure out how to alternate them and try to keep everybody involved. And I guess I should think more carefully about a "Plan B" when I am teaching something that relies on going outdoors.

MENTOR: That sounds like a good plan!

Dialogue: Guiding Questions

After you are done reading the conversation, discuss it with another mentor, or reflect upon your ability to identify and reflect back to the mentee the things you heard and saw in the lesson. Identify whether or not you observed issues similar to those in the example. List the guiding questions you heard, then talk about your perception of the effectiveness of the guiding questions.

For some mentors, guiding questions come to mind easily. However, for others, it may take practice to let go of the need to tell mentees what to do and develop the ability to ask about what happened in a nonthreatening way (Canning 1991). Mentors can use the following types of sample questions and statements as a starting point for helping their mentees reflect on their teaching following an observation (see Figure 2.2).

Beginning Guiding Questions
(for Post-Observation Conversation)

How do you feel about today's lesson?

How do you think it went today?

Did you accomplish what you set out to do today?

What were you expecting from today's lesson?

What have you been working on?

What can I help you with?

What in today's lesson would you like to talk about?

Figure 2.2

If these questions do not lead mentees to reflect upon the observation and areas for growth, mentors can move to the second level of questions (see Figure 2.3), which aim to extend a mentee's thinking and reflection by focusing more on areas that may need development.

Questions to Extend Mentee Thinking and Reflection

Can you tell me more about that?

Why do you think that happened?

What does the students' work tell you?

What about the students' behavior leads you to think that?

How else might you do that?

Figure 2.3

If a mentee still is not aware of what occurred in the classroom during the observation, or is aware of what occurred but is not sure how to change the situation, mentors can ask more direct questions, as demonstrated in the third category of questions (see Figure 2.4). These questions can help to direct the conversation toward areas of growth by showing the correlation between relationships or offering suggestions regarding areas of concern.

Questions to Direct Mentee Reflection More Specifically

I wonder what would happen if you tried _____?
(insert suggestion)

What do you think would happen if you did _____?
(insert suggestion)

Does this _____ relate to _____?
(insert mentee's action)   (insert student behavior)

How might _____ affect _____?
(insert mentee's action)   (insert students' behavior)

Figure 2.4

When mentors provide mentees with a true portrait of what happens in the classroom, mentees can then revise their actions, methods, or lessons to improve teaching. Though mentors must remain objective, they are not taking a passive role—they are providing new teachers with the tools needed for reflection that will last throughout the mentee's career.

Two Blackline masters are provided on the pages that follow:
• Expectations for the Mentee
• Expectations for the Mentor Teacher
You may use them to help define the mentoring relationship and the expectations you have for both the mentor and the mentee in a mentoring relationship.

Expectations for the Mentee

The following list identifies expectations for the mentee in the mentoring relationship. Review the list and select five key expectations that are critical for a successful mentoring relationship that meets the needs of the mentee.

The mentee will

1. come to the first year of teaching exhibiting enthusiasm, a love for learning, and a genuine liking for young people.

2. be open to developing a relationship with the mentor.

3. be willing to try new ideas and suggestions offered by the mentor.

4. bring to the experience ideas for topics and subjects that he or she would like to incorporate in his or her teaching.

5. bring to the experience a solid knowledge base.

6. bring to the experience a willingness to work hard.

7. get to know the facilities, personnel, environment, and political structure of the school.

8. be willing to create an interactive classroom via discussion groups, cooperative learning lessons, and by engaging students in higher-order questions, projects, and activities.

9. develop lesson plans that reflect varying formats.

10. develop and articulate a classroom management plan.

11. develop flexible lesson plans that can change when schedules and student needs dictate.

12. develop lesson plans that break down a concept and create a process for teaching it.

13. identify objectives for the day/lesson (on board/verbally/in lesson plan) and share objectives with students.

14. implement a variety of assessment strategies.

15. commit to teach a unit that they develop, without relying on a text.

16. identify his or her own learning style and explore how his or her learning style impacts his or her teaching.

(continued on next page)

Blackline 2.1

SkyLight Professional Development

17. observe teachers from a variety of subject areas and varying grade levels.

18. plan lessons that engage students of varying degrees of ability.

19. get involved in the total school experience, via extracurricular activities and all teacher duties, meetings, etc.

20. communicate with the mentor teacher daily.

21. exhibit a strong presence—the ability to stand up in front of the room and capture and hold student interest.

22. address the various learning styles and multicultural identities of his or her students.

Other Expectations

_____

_____

_____

_____

_____

_____

_____

_____

_____

_____

Top Five Critical Expectations — Key Words

\# ☐ _____

\# ☐ _____

\# ☐ _____

\# ☐ _____

\# ☐ _____

Blackline 2.1 (continued)

Expectations for the Mentor Teacher

The following list identifies expectations for the mentor teacher in the mentoring relationship. Review the list and select five key expectations that are critical for a successful mentoring relationship that addresses the needs of the mentee.

The mentor teacher will

1. communicate his or her expectations and objectives for the student teacher/first-year teacher at the start of the mentoring relationship.

2. allow the mentee to develop his or her own teaching style.

3. (for student teachers) assist the mentee in developing a schedule that identifies the gradual induction process (e.g., one class one week, adding a class and prep on a weekly basis; or two classes of the same prep that can be repeated later in the day, allowing for the mentor teacher to model a class that will be taught by the student teacher).

4. review the mentee's management plan and inform the mentee of school and district discipline policies.

5. arrange for release time to team teach with the mentee early in the semester/year.

6. arrange for introductions to other staff members, administrators, and school personnel.

7. maintain confidentiality.

8. arrange/encourage observations in other classes, levels of ability, and grade levels.

9. arrange for the principal to observe the mentee in a nonevaluative mode.

10. arrange for social interactions with the mentee.

11. identify his or her own learning style and discuss with the mentee how this style impacts his or her teaching.

12. provide an opportunity for the mentee to videotape his or her teaching both early and late in the semester/year.

13. encourage the mentee to implement a variety of curricular, teaching, and assessment strategies.

14. model infusion of multiculturalism on a daily basis (beyond the curriculum, as a part of life in the school).

15. model instruction that is differentiated for students with varying needs.

16. create a schedule than ensures communication with the mentee on a daily basis.

17. model effective interpersonal communication skills (in parent conferences, with administration and other faculty, and with students).

18. talk with mentee about career paths, discuss his or her goals and plans for the future.

(continued on next page)

Blackline 2.2

Addressing the Needs of the Mentee

19. discuss the legal issues of education with the mentee.

20. provide mentee with information on state requirements and mandates and describe processes in place for meeting these expectations in the classroom.

21. be aware of what is going on in the mentee's classroom by observing on a regular basis.

22. provide evidence of the mentee's classroom interactions and teaching strategies to the mentee following observations.

23. review lesson plans (check written plan and/or have mentee rehearse, discuss, or visualize).

24. provide the mentee with the opportunity to develop and teach his or her own curricular materials.

25. review the observational tool that will be used.

26. offer suggestions in areas requested by the mentee.

27. share curricular materials.

28. confer with the supervisor as needed.

29. serve as advocate when issues or concerns become problematic.

Other Expectations

_____

_____

_____

Top Five Critical Expectations — Number and Key Words

#☐ _____

#☐ _____

#☐ _____

#☐ _____

#☐ _____

Blackline 2.2 (continued)

In order to have important conversations that can lead to improved teaching and a higher level of learning for students, mentors and mentees must develop a trusting relationship built on open communication.

The Heart of Mentoring
Trust and Open Communication

by **Debra Pitton**

Open Communication

Open communication is necessary to build trust, but trust is necessary for open communication to occur. This endless loop makes it difficult for mentors to know where to begin their focus when they are working with a mentee. It is important that mentors remember that this process is not linear, but circular, and as such a starting point is needed. Mentors can establish trust more easily while working to communicate openly if some ground rules are established for interactions. While the term *ground rules* may sound negative and perhaps unnecessary, communication conflicts can be avoided with a plan for approaching conversations. Mentors can use the guidelines in Figure 3.1 for their ground rules or create their own to fit the needs of their mentoring relationship. These ground rules can be a starting point for developing trust and open communication.

Ground rules state publicly what both partners will do for each other. The commitment to these rules provides a solid base from which trust can be developed and open communication can occur.

Adapted from *Mentoring Novice Teachers* by D. Pitton, pp. 41–50. © 2000 by SkyLight Training and Publishing.

The Heart of Mentoring: Trust and Open Communication

Ground Rules for Mentor and Mentee

Mentor_____   Mentee_____

Ground rules apply to both parties.

1. Honesty is key. We need to say what we are feeling and thinking when we talk to each other.

2. Ask questions. If you are not sure about what has been said, ask "What do you mean?" Avoid filling in the blanks with your own interpretation—ask for clarification.

3. Create and stick to a schedule. Regular, planned times for conversation, observation, and informal get-togethers are vital to developing the relationship.

4. Respect the other's needs. It is okay to let the other person know that the timing of an unplanned conversation is not the best. But always set up a time in the near future for a phone call or conference to discuss the issue, and follow up on all concerns in a timely fashion.

Signed by: _____ and _____   Date: _____
            (mentor)   (mentee)

Figure 3.1

Open communication is based on honesty and takes into consideration the use of verbal, nonverbal, and paralinguistic interactions. Mentees sense that their mentors are truthful from the words that they use (verbal), the physical expressions and body language they exhibit (nonverbal), and the tone and inflection of their voice (paralinguistic). Messages are sent when individuals communicate, but the meaning of those messages is only perceived in the mind of the individual who hears the message (Hamilton with Parker 1990). While no mentor intentionally sends his or her mentee mixed signals, often not enough attention is paid to the use of verbal, nonverbal, and paralinguistic messages, and miscommunication results, obscuring the effectiveness of the mentor/mentee relationship.

Verbal Messages

Verbal messages are often considered to be the most accurate part of a dialogue between two people. How can spoken words be misinterpreted? Yet individuals cannot be sure that the verbal messages they send are actually what is heard by the listener. One married couple, for example, often checks signals on the amount of gas left in the car before the other uses it. If the woman hears from her husband, "There is enough gas to get you there," she interprets that to mean that she has at least a quarter of a tank. However, many times after hearing this from her husband she has found the needle on the gas gauge to be near empty. The woman may feel that her husband is not giving her a straight answer, but according to his view he is telling her the truth. He believes that even if the gas indicator is near empty, there is enough gas to get her to most places she wants to go. This is his interpretation of enough gas. The woman, however, does not have the same understanding of enough gas. Over time, this couple has come to understand that they mean very different things when they say or hear the words, "There is enough gas." Their awareness of the other's understanding of the words has enabled them to prevent conflict. This example demonstrates that individuals in any relationship need to carefully check signals to be sure that what is said is what is heard by the other party.

Mentors can read the following conversation to analyze the impact of verbal signals in communication.

Scenario: Focus on a Verbal Message

Ask two people to read the exchange between a novice teacher and a mentor while you listen. After you have "heard" the exchange, list the ways that the verbal message (words only) could be interpreted by the mentee.

Mentor:	Hi, Sam. I found it really interesting observing you in class today. I'm glad we can take some time to discuss what went on.
Mentee:	Yeah, things didn't go exactly as I had planned.
Mentor:	Let's talk about that. What did you plan and how did the actual lesson vary from that plan?
Mentee:	My goal was to have the kids explore the various properties of paper by having them feel the paper, write on it, tear it, and soak it in water—and I had a whole bunch of different types of paper for them to use. I had waxed paper, construction paper, cardboard, typing paper, notebook paper, toilet paper, and paper towels.

Mentor: There was a lot for them to explore.

Mentee: Yeah—maybe too much. They were so busy doing the tearing and soaking that they didn't write down any of their discoveries.

Mentor: I didn't hear any of the directions you gave the students.

Mentee: Well, it was a discovery lesson.

Mentor: Discovery? Hmmmm.

Mentee: We learned about teaching by discovery in my methods class at the university.

Mentor: Do you think that a discovery lesson fit what you were trying to do?

Dialogue: Misinterpretation

Debrief with a colleague or write out your answers. What are the various ways that the words used by the mentor could be misinterpreted? What about the word choices of the mentee? Try rewriting this dialogue using different word choices to see if you can find some language that is clearer to the listener. Ask two people to read the dialogue again, so you can practice listening to your word choices and their possible implications.

Some mentors who analyzed this conversation came up with these suggestions for clarifying the verbal message:

- Using the word *interesting* to describe the lesson might be interpreted negatively by the mentee. A simple "Thanks for letting me hang out in your class today" might be a better beginning, as it does not allow for misinterpretation.

- The question "What did you plan . . . ?" is supportive because it suggests that the mentee actually did have a plan.

- The words *Discovery? Hmmmm,* might be interpreted as a negative comment through which the mentor indicates this is not something he or she cares for, or it might be interpreted as an inquisitive comment. In

SkyLight Professional Development

GUIDEBOOK

either case, the word choice is open to misinterpretation by the mentee.

- The statement "Well, it was a discovery lesson," made by the mentee might seem to be justifying his or her decision.

This role-play demonstrates that mentors need to think about their word choices to make sure they are not being misconstrued. For example, to clarify meaning after using the word *interesting* in the dialogue, the mentor might have said, "I am always amazed by all the various methods that can be used in the classroom." This kind of explanation can help avoid misinterpretation.

There is no way for individuals to be absolutely sure that what they say is interpreted by the listener in the way they intended it. Therefore, it is important that mentors check signals by asking questions when they are not sure about what they have heard, and it is equally important that mentors are sure their mentees heard their words the way they intended. If mentors think they might have heard something incorrectly, they need to ask, "So you are saying that . . . ?" or "Do you mean . . . ?" to check the accuracy of their interpretation. Without checking signals, mentors may have a false impression of what occurred in the classroom or an inaccurate view of what mentees think. If mentors have a trusting relationship with their mentees, it is easier for them to ask their mentees if they are comfortable with the communication that took place, and be sure they have gotten an honest answer.

Another way mentors can avoid misinterpretation is to give the lead to their mentees. For example, when first talking to mentees about a classroom observation, mentors should not qualify what they have seen by giving it any descriptors. Mentors can make a statement such as "Thanks for giving me the opportunity to see students in action" or "I appreciate you letting me spend time in your class." Mentees are usually eager to know if mentors liked the lesson or not; thus, a mentor's initial comments may be interpreted as a statement of "like" or "dislike" toward what happened in the classroom. A mentor's

The Heart of Mentoring: Trust and Open Communication

lead-in statement should not give a mentee any indicator of his or her feelings. Lead-in statements should be emotionally neutral, so mentors do not inadvertently send a signal to their mentees that interferes with the discussion. If mentees think their mentor did not like their lesson, they may become defensive and unable to hear the mentor's comments and suggestions. On the other hand, if mentees think their mentor liked the lesson, they may discount the mentor's suggestions. The use of statements such as "That was interesting," "That was nice," or "Wow, I'd be worn out after that class," are vague and can be misinterpreted by an anxious beginner. It is easy to imagine a novice teacher thinking, "An interesting class? What does that mean? Was it too rowdy? Is she saying *interesting* because she doesn't want to be critical? Was it interesting because there was so much going on that needs to be fixed?" A neutral lead-in serves as a transition from the actual lesson to the conversation that concerns the lesson.

As mentors and mentees work at open communication, having ground rules is useful as mentors can refer to them and ask their mentees if they are clear about what was said. If ground rules are established that say that both mentors and mentees will work to be open and honest with each other, and that both parties need to clarify if something is not clear, a reference point for checking signals is established. Mentors can work toward open communication by saying something such as, "In our ground rules we agreed to be open with each other. So, I would really like it if you would let me know if there is anything I said that is confusing to you or that doesn't seem to connect with what you are thinking."

Mentors can further investigate the importance of checking signals through the following exercise.

Dialogue: Exact Language

Ask another mentor or mentee (or even a family member or friend) to list what they mean when they say the following statements, and then answer the questions yourself. Next, share your interpretations with each other. What did you learn about yourself and the person you exchanged lists with regarding your individual understanding of the words? How can you use this knowledge in your work with your mentee?

What do you mean when you say these sentences (be as specific as possible)?
- I'll be there in a few minutes.
- Can I borrow a couple of bucks?
- Can I borrow some money?
- Come here a second.
- I'll be right there.
- It needs some work.
- It's okay.
- I've done that lots of times.

When you use these words, what do they mean to you?
- Sometimes
- Always
- Never
- Usually
- Maybe

This exercise demonstrates how important it is to use exact language to help avoid misinterpretation. If, for example, a mentor states that his or her mentee never gets the students refocused after a disruption, the imprecise language may create a barrier as the mentee might think, "It's not true that I never get the students refocused." The mentor might have used the word *never* for impact or just failed to consider how the word might be interpreted. "That was good," "I liked that," and "That needs some work" are all statements that do not use exact language. Mentors can prevent misinterpretation by telling the mentee specifically what was good, exactly what occurred in the classroom that they liked and why, and identifying what needs some work. By being specific, communication can be much more accurate and effective.

Nonverbal Messages

Many people have probably heard the statement, "It's not what you said, it's how you said it." This statement exemplifies how the nonverbal components of communication must be considered as well as the verbal. Nonverbal signals include facial expressions, vocal tone, inflection, and body stance. It is important that nonverbal messages match verbal messages, as people often tend to pay more attention to these signals than to words.

People's faces and bodies often reveal what they are feeling, even if their words do not. If someone frowns as she tells her guest that she is glad he dropped by to visit, the guest gets the message that she is really not very pleased to see him. If a person lowers his eyes and looks away as he tells a colleague that he likes her idea, she may get the message that he is not sincere. Listeners add meaning to the messages they hear as they make sense of the words and interpret nonverbal signals. Sending contradicting verbal and nonverbal signals is a common cause of miscommunication. Mentors can communicate more accurately by being aware of nonverbal messages.

Vocal tone is a component of nonverbal language called *paralanguage,* and it is what is remembered more than the actual words used when a person speaks. According to research by George Trager (1958), vocal tone is what occurs in conversations beyond or in addition to the words we speak. The match or mismatch between what is said and the tone used is very important in conversations. If the tone matches the words, the message is believable; if the tone is not congruent with the words, it is the tone that delivers the message.

It is important that mentors match their tone to their verbal message. If a mentor tells her mentee that she wants to support him, but uses a contradictory or inconsistent tone when uttering the words, the words will not be heard by the mentee. For example, if a mentor tells a mentee that he likes the way she called on her students in class, but he says it hesitantly while looking away, the mentor sends a nonverbal cue that he does not necessarily mean what his words convey. Mentors can try the following exercises to heighten their awareness of nonverbal communication and the use of paralanguage.

Dialogue: Nonverbal Practice 1

Say the following phrases to another mentor or videotape yourself. Try to convey the positive emotion listed in the parentheses. If you are using a videotape, watch your physical stances, gestures, and facial expressions and listen to your verbal tone when you play back the video. If you are having another mentor watch you, have your partner reflect back to you what they see in your face and body and what tone and voice they hear. Answer the questions at the end of the exercise. The goal is to get a sense of how you convey these emotions.

- I think you're doing a great job! (enthusiasm)
- When you said that to the student, what was their response? (thoughtfulness)
- The class was on task, even if they were a bit loud. (confidence)
- I know it's hard to find time to create your lesson plans. (support)
- Do you want me to give you some suggestions? (questioning)
- I really enjoyed watching the students interact in their small groups yesterday. (pleased)
- It's tough when a parent gets angry with you. (empathy)
- I saw what you did with the fourth grade math lesson on fractions yesterday. (awe)

Follow-up questions:
- From your observations or the feedback you received, how would you describe how your nonverbal signals matched your messages?
- What might you need to do to change your tone, facial expressions, or body language to more accurately reflect the words you are speaking?

Mentors who discussed the questions following the dialogue exercise above identified that it was not always easy to match their vocal tone and nonverbal signals. They noted that having an awareness of their use of tone and the ways in which they created the tone they wanted was important. By listening to themselves and working with peers, these mentors felt they were able to monitor their own use of tone and nonverbal signals to create accurate messages when they communicated. Mentors agree that it is important to convey confidence to mentees, even if there is some doubt in the mentor's mind about the novice teacher's capabilities, and the vocal tone is very important when conveying confidence. If mentees hear mentors tell them they are improving, but hear uncertainty in the mentor's voice, they probably will not believe the mentor. This leads mentees to have a lack of confidence in themselves, and to begin to distrust their mentor. Mentees expect honesty, and if they get a sense that their mentor does not mean what they say, the relationship is negatively impacted.

Mentors can engage in the following dialogue exercise to identify nonverbal and paralinguistic signals that go with negative emotions. By becoming aware of the signals of these emotions, mentors can work to avoid them.

Dialogue: Nonverbal Practice 2

Practice saying the phrases listed below using the identified negative emotion and accompanying nonverbal signals. Videotape yourself or have another mentor provide feedback. This exercise strengthens your awareness of the tone, stance, gestures, and facial expressions that accompany negative emotions, so you can monitor your own interactions to avoid inadvertently sending a message that you do not intend.

- I think you're doing a great job. (hesitancy)
- When you said that to the student, what was their response? (anger)
- The class was on task, even if they were a bit loud. (sarcastic)
- I know it's hard to find time to create your lesson plans. (unbelieving)
- Do you want me to give you some suggestions? (demanding)
- I really enjoyed watching the students interact in their small groups yesterday. (sarcastic)
- It's tough when a parent gets angry with you. (unconcerned)
- I saw what you did with the fourth grade math lesson on fractions yesterday. (disbelief)

Follow-up questions:
- What did you pay more attention to, the words or the emotion (nonverbal message) of each phrase?
- How would you feel if you heard these messages (and tone)?
- What could you do to create a more positive tone/emotion to match these verbal and nonverbal messages?

The reflection questions following the phrases identify the contradiction that occurs when a person says words that by themselves might seem positive, but are reflected using a negative tone and body language. When this happens, the listener often focuses on the emotion conveyed in such a contradictory message.

It is important that mentors practice matching their tone to the words they speak, especially when conversing with a mentee. Awareness of tone, facial expression, and body language helps the mentor match verbal and nonverbal messages. Mentors can use a mirror or practice with a friend to increase their ability to monitor their tone and nonverbal messages.

Nonverbal communication also includes factors such as the distance people stand from one another as they speak, eye contact, the way people take turns talking, how people listen, and when people choose to communicate. Some of these aspects of communication are cultural and some are gender based (Samovar, Porter, and Jain 1981). If a mentee and mentor do not share the same cultural background, it is important that the mentor think carefully about these differences. During the getting-acquainted process at the beginning of the mentoring relationship, it is critical that both parties talk about how they communicate, and perhaps also include diverse communication perspectives in the ground rules. For example, during an initial conversation with a mentee, mentors should identify their personal preferences for communication and ask the mentee to share what their preferences are. A mentor might say, "I really find that I like to think about an issue for a while before I am ready to decide what to do about the problem. I know that some of my colleagues like to jump right in with solutions, but I like to mull things over. So, I may be very quiet about things while I am thinking. This doesn't mean that I am not happy about what I have observed or what we are discussing, it just means I am thinking. I wanted you to know that so you can get a sense of my communication style. What about you? How do you like to approach issues?"

Mentors who often react with intense emotions, speak loudly and with authority, or are aware that they really do not like to spend a lot of time hashing over an issue should communicate these things to their mentee. Mentees may use or prefer other communication styles, and mentors need to be aware of these differences to set up ground rules that identify and validate these differences in communication styles.

In addition, mentors should keep in mind that various patterns of communication have been described as gender related. For example, Deborah Tannehill (1989) states that male communication responses to a problem often include specific ideas for solving the issue, while female communication responses lean more toward nurturing and empathic statements. These patterns need to be explored to determine if they reflect the individuals involved, and mentors should definitely consider these patterns if they have a different problem-solving style than their mentees.

The following aspects of nonverbal communication identify a European-American cultural perspective and the impact these components may have on a conversation. These components should be given attention in all mentoring relationships. Mentors who are mentoring someone with different cultural communication standards should explore these aspects of intercultural communication. Mentors can start by asking their mentees about their comfort level with the following aspects of communication.

Proximity

As everyone has a certain comfort level with the personal space that surrounds them, standing too close to another during conversation can create discomfort for a person. In a situation where a mentee may perceive the mentor as having more power (e.g., in a student teaching situation), standing too close while talking may heighten the sense of dominance. This is not productive when trying to develop trust.

Turn-Taking

A speaker who does not allow someone to complete what he or she is saying, but rather jumps in with comments or suggestions, can give the impression of not caring if he or she hears what the other person is saying. Interrupting someone minimizes his or her contributions to the conversation. In open communication, each member of the conversation has an equal right to speak, and taking turns is important. Mentoring is not about one person telling the other what to do—it is about sharing information to reach conclusions about educational practice.

Eye Contact

Most Americans expect people to look them in the eye when they talk to them, and if the listener looks away, the speaker may perceive a lack of interest. On the other hand, when someone stares at another person with an intense gaze, it can be disarming as well. Mentors should strive to use the appropriate level of eye contact to reflect their interest and support when speaking with their mentees.

Listening

There is a listening stance that communicates that someone is paying attention to what is being said in a conversation. A person who is leaning forward and concentrating on what the speaker is saying signals that he or she is listening. Another aspect of listening is balance in the conversation. Mentors need to keep this in mind, giving their mentees plenty of opportunities to talk about what is happening in their classrooms.

Use of Time

Allowing significant time for a conversation to occur is another signal that the message is important. If mentors set up a time to talk with their mentees and then frequently change the meeting time or look at their watches and seem eager to get going,

The Heart of Mentoring: Trust and Open Communication

mentees may feel that what they have to say is not valued. This undermines trust and prohibits open communication.

By paying attention to the process of communication, mentors can develop trust and provide for open dialogue with their mentees. Without trust and open communication little is accomplished because the mentee will not share important issues or concerns. In order to have important discussions that can lead to improved teaching and higher levels of learning for students, mentors must pay attention to these components of their relationship with their mentees.

REFERENCES

Hamilton, C., with C. Parker. 1990. *Communicating for results.* Belmont, CA: Wadsworth.

Samovar, L., R. Porter, and N. Jain, 1981. *Understanding intercultural communication.* Belmont, CA: Wadsworth.

Tannehill, D. 1989. Student teaching: A view from the other side. *Journal of Teaching in Physical Education.* 8: 243–253.

Trager, G. 1958. Paralanguage: A first approximation. *Studies in Linguistics.* 13: 1–12.

Planning the Itinerary

Jan—
These techniques work
great in class. Let's
get together next week
and talk!

Sharon

Janice Langley
234 S. Cedar St.
Minton, VT 02234

10¢ BLUE SPRUCE

5¢ Seagull

If mentoring is to serve as a viable process in the midst of change, we must focus on how a person can become a mentor and be a mentor, as opposed to simply doing mentoring (Sullivan 1992, p. 1).

 entoring is more than showing a new teacher around a school or giving him old lesson plans and tests. A mentor serves as a formal guide who plans the educational itinerary with the protégé. The new teacher, of course, is free to embark on individual journeys, but the mentor helps the protégé and the students visit important destinations such as objectives, standards, and academic goals along the way. Trust in a mentoring relationship may form the foundation of a strong partnership, but the new teacher also needs to know how to plan lessons, design units, and manage a classroom. Allowing the new teacher to learn by trial and error is not always appropriate for effective teaching and optimal student learning. Since the first weeks of school establish a pattern, presenting effective lessons and units and organizing the classroom are critical components that need to be discussed and planned *prior* to the start of school.

In Selection 4, Jan Skowron provides templates to help protégés plan a lesson design that correlates to standards and provides a description of what students must demonstrate in order to show they have met or exceeded the standards. New teachers often need help in developing the components of an effective lesson plan, even though their pre-service training may have included some information. Often, undergraduates spend weeks in a college course planning curriculum. The reality of planning four or five lessons each day in most schools overwhelms many new teachers; moreover, ineffective lesson planning can result in a disastrous beginning for students and teachers. Protégés may need help to create motivating lesson hooks, select appropriate teaching strategies, group students, and assess student work. One of the most critical decisions teachers make every day is determining what type of learning activities will help students achieve deep understanding of the content. The decision to use graphic organizers, role-play scenarios, or create projects is important because various strategies meet the need of the diverse students.

A mentor serves as a formal guide who plans the educational itinerary with the protégé.

In addition to Skowron's model of planning individual lessons, I have developed a user-friendly process of planning an integrated curriculum unit that includes learning experiences and assessments from Howard Gardner's eight intelligences. Selection 5 shows how teachers can work in teams to brainstorm appropriate activities that help students learn and meet curriculum objectives and learning standards. The multiple intelligence grid serves as a template for planning two- to three-week units designed to motivate students as well as address multiple curriculum goals.

Even though a well-developed lesson or unit plan establishes the expectations for academic goals, students may not stay on task unless they know the expectations for their own behavior. Selection 6 reviews methods for establishing a classroom climate conducive for social interaction and learning. I advocate the responsibility model where students work together cooperatively and care about the welfare of others in their classroom community. I also stress the importance of developing procedures, rules, and consequences with the students during the first few days of school. When students have some input on decisions in their classroom, they are able to internalize the expectations and are more likely to adhere to the behavior standards they helped establish.

Inappropriate teacher behaviors or comments can erode a positive classroom climate and may threaten the environment of the classroom for the entire year. Beginning teachers may inadvertently say or do something that embarrasses, alienates, or angers a student. The damage from just one incident could be irreversible. In Selection 7, "Burke's Dirty Dozen" describes twelve types of behaviors teachers should avoid in order to prevent *causing* discipline problems. Proactive teachers prevent many behavior problems—or at least diffuse minor problems—before they escalate into more serious behavior disruptions. Protégés need to be forewarned about the toxic atmosphere that could permeate a classroom. Students who do not feel liked or respected often resort to inappropriate behavior in retaliation for their hurt feelings.

In Selection 8, Bellanca and Fogarty focus on teaching students how to interact socially before they move into cooperative groups and engage in meaningful performances or proj-

Trust in a mentoring relationship may form the foundation of a strong partnership, but the new teacher also needs to know how to plan lessons, design units, and manage a classroom.

The first year will be filled with near disasters, complete disasters, and tremendous triumphs that add to the emotional roller-coaster ride of teaching.

ects. If students possess the proper social skills for group interaction before the group begins working, many behavior problems can be avoided. Bellanca and Fogarty suggest teachers create lessons that reinforce the importance of using appropriate social skills. Behavior problems usually begin with a whimper—not a bang! Little irritants like talking out of turn or making silly noises aggravate new teachers and often cause them to overreact because they are trying to show the students that they are in charge. Beginning teachers can easily escalate a minor disruption into a major power struggle if they say or do the wrong thing and alienate one or two students or the entire class. Unfortunately, some teachers abandon cooperative group work or engaging projects altogether instead of taking the time to teach and assess appropriate interpersonal skills.

Selection 9 explores some practical strategies to use with students to prevent minor problems from becoming major problems. I offer a variety of techniques to deal with students who seek attention, power, and revenge, as well as students who demonstrate aggressive behaviors or students who feel inadequate. I have also included several problem-solving scenarios with some possible resolutions that new teachers can try before resorting to outside help. Both veteran and new teachers should develop a repertoire of strategies to address the needs of their diverse students while maintaining an educational atmosphere conducive for optimal learning.

Of course, every journey has its share of misadventures, lost luggage, and poor accommodations. Like any traveler, the new teacher will also experience many challenges during the first year's journey. The first year will be filled with near disasters, complete disasters, and tremendous triumphs that make teaching such an emotional roller-coaster ride. The wise mentor provides a thoughtful itinerary of lesson plan designs, unit designs, social skills, lessons, and classroom management strategies to make the journey more enjoyable and fulfilling, not only for the new teacher but also for the students.

REFERENCES

Sullivan, C. G. 1992. *How to mentor in the midst of change*. Alexandria, VA: Association for Supervision and Curriculum Development.

Good teaching begins with a thoughtful lesson plan designed to integrate appropriate activities, resources, and assessments to achieve the desired results for students. Often, mentors must introduce mentees to instructional design and lesson planning. Mentors can use the basic design plan to help mentees begin with the end in mind.

Basic Instructional Design

by **Jan Skowron**

The Basic Instructional Design Planning Guide is a thinking process approach to guide decision making for basic instructional planning. It is comprised of three sections: (1) Desired Results, (2) Lesson Design, and (3) Evidence of Learning. Each of the three sections includes three columns: Planning Questions and Decisions, Information and Data Sources, and Notes and Comments. The Planning Questions and Decisions column poses a series of key questions to guide and stimulate thinking during the planning process. The Information and Data Sources column lists the types of resources and data sources that will facilitate answering the questions in column one. The Notes and Comments column provides information that will further clarify and assist in answering questions in column one. A detailed explanation of each section follows.

Adapted from *Powerful Lesson Planning Models* by J. Skowron, pp. 11–23, 31–32. © 2001 by SkyLight Training and Publishing.

MENTORING

PLANNING GUIDE–BASIC INSTRUCTION
SECTION 1: DESIRED RESULTS
Use these questions to plan a basic instructional design.

PLANNING QUESTIONS AND DECISIONS	INFORMATION AND DATA SOURCES	NOTES AND COMMENTS
1. What learning standards/ benchmarks will be taught?	District curriculum guides, district and state standards documents, student needs based on test data (formal and informal), school improvement goals, district goals, state initiatives	A decision regarding what is to be taught is made before completing the rest of the planning process.
2. What is the specific learning standard?	_____	A clear statement of what students are to do provides clarity and focus in planning.
3. What assessment activities will enable students to demonstrate they have met the learning standard?	Recommended and required assessments, textbook materials	Planning for assessment is a recursive process. Assessment strategies and tools are tentatively outlined in the initial stages of instructional design, reconsidered and modified as the design emerges, and then finalized as the design is completed.
4. What performance expectations are there for students to show the extent of learning that has occurred?	District, state expectations for performance and/or teacher developed expectations	
5. How will students' difficulties be recognized along the way?	Formative assessments, observational techniques	
6. What assessment materials are available and what materials need to be developed?	Rubrics and assessments in district curriculum guides, teacher manuals, other sources	
7. How will assessment results be communicated to students and parents?	Report cards, grading scale, narrative report, conference, portfolio	Select the assessment strategy that is most appropriate. If the assessment results are to be incorporated into a grade, appropriate documentation should be made.

Figure 4.1

(continued on next page)

Section 1: Desired Results

Learning Standards

The process of instructional design begins with the learning standards—what students are expected to know and do (see Figure 4.1). It is this desired end result that drives the planning process and provides the focus and direction for the lesson. Wiggins and McTighe (1998) tell us to begin with the end in mind—think first about the desired results.

SkyLight Professional Development

SECTION 1: DESIRED RESULTS
Planning Questions and Decisions

Science Class Grade 7

1. What learning standards/benchmarks will be taught?
The standard is part of the district curriculum in physical science and part of the sequence in understanding solutions. It aligns to state and NSTA standards.

2. What is the specific learning standard?
Students will distinguish between mixtures that are solutions and those that are not.

3. What assessment activities will enable students to demonstrate they have met the learning standard?
Students will enter findings and conclusions in their science log. A forced choice assessment will show what factual knowledge students have acquired. (I may modify the assessment to include additional information.) Students will develop an outline for their presentation. (The presentation rubric will be used.)

4. What performance expectations are there for students to show the extent of learning that has occurred?
Science logs will have appropriate detail and diagrams. (Corrections are expected if necessary.) Students will answer 80% of the questions on the forced choice test correctly. (Corrections are expected if necessary.) Students will develop an outline for their presentation. (The presentation rubric will be used.)

5. How will students' difficulties be recognized along the way?
Student responses during class discussion will be noted to determine understanding. (I need to ask several questions during class discussion to ascertain students' understanding. I will use my class list to note which students appear to need further assistance. They will be paired with a "stronger partner" for a study buddies activity.)

6. What assessment materials are available and what materials need to be developed?
Instructions for the experiments and a rubric describing levels of performance for the science log entries will be developed and discussed prior to the lesson.

7. How will assessment results be communicated to students and parents?
Students will receive a copy of the rubric showing the assessment of their science log with teacher comments. Students will understand that the science log assessment and the forced choice test will be included in their quarterly report card grade.

Figure 4.1 (continued)

Objective Objection

Educators may state learning benchmarks (objectives) in such precise terms that they become confused with activities. A clear distinction and an obvious connection exists between a benchmark and an activity. The benchmark is what the student will know and be able to do as a result of engaging in the activity. Start with the standard or benchmark, determine what evidence to acquire to assess whether the standard or benchmark is met, and plan the activities to get to this end.

Section 2: Lesson Design

A lesson plan is what the teacher does to teach the learning standard (see Figure 4.4). The components of a lesson plan are described below (see also Figure 4.2).

Opening

The opening of the lesson sets the stage for what is to follow. The "anticipation" that is created motivates students and peaks their interest (Hunter 1984). It activates students' schemata by tapping into their prior knowledge and making connections to new learning. Calling to mind what is already known is critical for learning. Jensen (2000) says that the more associations and connections one makes, the more firmly new information is "woven in neurologically." There is greater depth of meaning when new information is connected to existing knowledge. The lesson opening, therefore, should be structured to help students recall what they already know, understand the relevance of what they will learn, and be aware of what they will know and be able to do as a result of the learning activity. In other words, students should consciously connect new learning to previous learning. The teacher facilitates this process through appropriate opening activities.

COMPONENTS OF AN EFFECTIVE LESSON PLAN

- Opening
- Teaching strategies/activities (input)
- Student activities
- Materials/resources
- Grouping pattern
- Monitoring student progress
- Ending/summary/reflection
- Practice activities/assignments

Figure 4.2

Teaching Strategies/Activities (Input)

Teaching strategies are selected based on the type of content to be taught and the needs and abilities of the students. They include demonstrating, modeling, explaining, questioning, and coaching. Teaching strategies are what the teacher does to develop background and set the stage for the learning activities students will engage in. The input provided at this point gives students enough information to proceed confidently with the learning tasks (see Figure 4.3). It does not preclude exploration and discovery on their part.

CONTENT-SPECIFIC EXAMPLES OF TEACHING INPUT

- Demonstrating pulley operation
- Modeling a think-aloud during a poetry reading
- Explaining the life cycle of a frog
- Questioning and discussing to elicit higher-order thinking related to legislative decisions
- Coaching for sound articulation

Figure 4.3

Student Activities

In selecting or developing an instructional activity it is important to consider its "fit" with the learning standard and student needs and abilities. An instructional activity is always related to the learning standard—it is not an end in itself. To learn, a student engages in an activity. A learning activity may be as simple as reading a selection, or it may be a more complex activity such as gathering data from multiple sources for problem solving. Today, a plethora of instructional activities are offered in teaching manuals, professional journals, books, newsletters, software, and the Internet. Far more activities are available than can possibly be used. The teacher must be selective.

Engaged Learning How students learn is just as important as what they learn. Student engagement is a high-priority in instructional design. Danielson (1996, 95) states: "Engaging students in learning is the raison d'etre of education. All other components are in the service of student engagement . . .". But engaged learning activities are not selected merely for their hands-on quality and potential for enjoyment. The purpose of engagement is to involve students in developing important concepts, skills, and processes. Engagement provides the condition in which concepts are made meaningful.

PLANNING GUIDE—BASIC INSTRUCTION
SECTION 2: DESIGN
Use these questions to plan a basic instructional design.

PLANNING QUESTIONS AND DECISIONS	INFORMATION AND DATA SOURCES	NOTES AND COMMENTS
1. What are the learning standards/ benchmarks to be achieved?	See Section 1: Desired Results.	
2. What is a motivating opening for the lesson?		
3. What strategies or activities will be used to teach the standard?	Curriculum guides, teaching manuals, professional literature, best practices information, etc. are sources of information for lesson development.	
4. What materials are needed to support and enhance learning?		
5. What is the appropriate use of technology?		
6. How will students be grouped for this activity?		
7. What opportunities will students have to reflect on their learning?		
8. How will student progress be monitored?		
9. What forms of additional practice may be necessary?		
10. How long will the lesson take?		
11. Are there any foreseeable pitfalls in this lesson?		
12. What alternatives are there if the lesson doesn't work out?		

Figure 4.4

(continued on next page)

Types of Learning Activities Learning activities are designed to enable students to reach specified standards. This is not as simple as it may sound. Other considerations affect the design of learning activities. Student interest impacts motivation, which affects attention and retention (Cummings 1980).

SECTION 2: LESSON DESIGN
Planing Questions and Decisions
Science Class Grade 7

1. What are the learning standards/benchmarks to be achieved?
Students will distinguish between mixtures that are solutions and those that are not.

2. What is a motivating opening for the lesson?
Set up as a problem-solving activity related to a real-life application: forensic scientist working with a detective to solve a criminal case. Show two containers of liquid and how they would identify the one that has water and the one that contains another substance. Ask students why such identification is necessary or important. Record responses for later review.

3. What strategies or activities will be used to teach the standard?
Possibilities include: Review and develop background information through discussion, reading, research, and questioning the teacher. Use KWL strategy. Invite a chemist from a local industry to talk with students about real-life applications. Conduct demonstration or experiment. Use lab record/report activity.

4. What materials are needed to support and enhance learning?
Safety goggles, lab aprons, graduated cylinders, clear plastic glasses or beakers, stirring rods, six prepared mixtures (water/milk, water/sugar, water/oil, water/rubbing alcohol, water/drink mix, sand/salt)
For Tyndall effect: Flashlight, cardboard, metric ruler, pencil

5. What is the appropriate use of technology?
Students may keep notes on word processing program. The computer probe equipment is also a possibility, perhaps as a demonstration.

6. How will students be grouped for this activity?
Students will work in groups of three for the lab experiment. The class as a whole will discuss findings and outcomes.

7. What opportunities will students have to reflect on their learning?
At the conclusion of the lesson, students will write on three new things they learned as a result of the lesson and how these three things have application to their everyday life. (This could be part of the assessment.)

8. How will student progress be monitored?
During lab work, the teacher will observe students and check for proper use of equipment and following directions. Spot checks of lab book entries will be made.

9. What forms of additional practice may be necessary?
Students who miss this session or need further input may review textbook diagrams and explanations of the Tyndall effect and solutions. A video disk segment on solutions may be viewed. Or, they could partner with another student to review science log entries.

10. How long will the lesson take?
Two class periods will be scheduled for this lesson. I may have to provide additional time to get all presentations in—or I could have just a few groups present. Other groups could present for other lessons.

11. Are there any foreseeable pitfalls in this lesson?
Students must perform the experiment carefully to obtain the desired results. Students will need teacher supervision and direction in carrying out the experiment to ensure safety and proper use of lab equipment. Extra mixtures will be available in case of spills.

12. What alternatives are there if the lesson doesn't work out?
A demonstration will be used if the student activity doesn't work out as planned. Students will observe and record their findings in their science logs.

Figure 4.4 (continued)

DESIGNING LEARNING ACTIVITIES

Literal Learning. Literal learning defines a relatively simple activity for acquiring basic information and facts. The following are examples of literal learning activities:
- Name the steps in the scientific method.
- Identify the President of the United States during the Great Depression.
- Match the Generals to their Civil War battles.
- Identify given rocks and minerals.

Relational Learning. In relational learning students relate or connect information from one or more sources including their own background knowledge. Some examples of relational learning activities are
- Locate the ancient civilization of Mesopotamia on a modern-day map.
- Compare the population of Illinois and Chicago over time.
- Predict the next action in a story.

Transformational Learning. Transformational learning requires the student to transcribe or apply learning in a different way. Some examples of transformational learning activities are as follows:
- Rewrite the ending to a story.
- Demonstrate the operation of a simple machine.
- Dramatize a historical event.

Extensional Learning. Extensional learning activities ask students to take their learning and extend it using literal, relational, and transformational strategies to create, produce, originate, evaluate, and in other ways exhibit their learning in a unique way. Some examples are
- Critique a novel.
- Design a rubric for a learning task and use it to assess the task.
- Justify the actions of the main character in a story.

Figure 4.5

Therefore learning activities should be appealing and interesting to students. An appropriate level of challenge is necessary to maintain interest; therefore learning activities should be designed to meet a wide range of student needs.

It is apparent that some learning standards relate to simple information and fact acquisition. Other standards require the learner to relate, transform, or extend concepts. The wording of the learning standard is a guide in developing learning activities. The wording of the learning activity guides the students in the learning task.

The categorization of learning into literal, relational, transformational, and extensional domains allows teachers to use the wording of state learning standards. The categories do overlap. Strictly defined, separate categories of learning activities may not be possible, but understanding general categories of learning helps to focus planning of activities in relation to the learning standards (see Figure 4.5). All students should participate in all types of learning. It would be a drastic mistake to treat these categories as a hierarchy in which students begin with literal learning, staying there until the teacher decides mastery is obtained, and then move on to the next category. Linear use of learning categories is neither indicated nor effective. It is contrary to theory and research, which suggests an overlap and integration of the various types of thinking (Good and Brophy 1997). It is not possible to totally isolate levels of thinking into separate compartments—they are interrelated and iterative (Ellis and Fouts 1997).

Describing Learning Activities A critical part of instructional planning is the description, explanation, or directions for a learning activity. The wording of the description is carefully chosen to convey precisely what students are to accomplish. Selecting appropriate terminology for the learning activity is necessary to design coherent and organized instruction. If the students are asked only to list events in chronological order, it is not fair to expect that they will analyze those events. If analysis behavior is expected, the terminology that conveys this expectation must be used. The key word in the description of an instructional activity is the linchpin and, therefore, must be carefully chosen. A list of suggested terms for learning activities is contained in Figure 4.6. Teachers may find it helpful to refer to this list in describing instructional activities.

Designing Learning Activities: Terms to Use

Use the following terms to help recognize the type of learning required in a standard and to design instructional activities that correspond to the learning standard.

Literal Learning

count	label	outline
define	list	quote
find	match	recall
identify	name	tell

Relational Learning

compare	differentiate	locate	restate
conclude	discuss	measure	review
contrast	explain	paraphrase	sequence
demonstrate	generalize	predict	show
describe	interpret	report	summarize

Transformational Learning

analyze	collect	diagram	rewrite
apply	compute	distinguish	select
change	debate	dramatize	separate
characterize	deduce	examine	use
choose	demonstrate	research	

Extensional Learning

appraise	criticize	judge	prioritize
assess	decide	justify	produce
choose	design	make up	propose
compose	develop	originate	prove
conclude	evaluate	perform	rank
construct	integrate	plan	rate
create	invent	pretend	

Figure 4.6

Basic Instructional Design

LEARNING ACTIVITIES

1. Graphic Organizers
Use graphic organizers to create mind maps for students, thereby strengthening learning and subsequent recall of material. When the graphic organizers are personalized to match the needs and backgrounds of the students, they become even more powerful. A slightly different twist is to use pictures or drawings instead of words to create a mind map.

2. Creative Retelling
Weave content information into a story using known genres such as fables, tall tales, songs, and myths. In this manner, the information is transformed into a different setting.

3. Peer Presenting
Use an "each one, teach one" model, or in some manner allow students to teach one another. Explaining strengthens understanding.

4. Model Making
Create models (two- or three-dimensional) to produce a concrete representation of an abstract concept.

5. Performance
Transform information or a concept into a performance using drama, music, or dance. Write about the solution to a math problem or create a poem about a science concept.

6. Role Playing
Provide opportunities for some students to assume the role of historical or fictional characters while other students take on the role of reporter in an interview activity that contributes to whole learning through a simulated experience.

Figure 4.7

(continued on next page)

Brain-Frame Activities Recent research into how the brain learns provides a rich source of information for teachers as they plan instruction. Teachers frame instruction around brain-compatible learning to maximize learning. Robin Fogarty (1997) tells us that brain-compatible classrooms differ from others in three major ways. First, brain-compatible learning is integrated, not isolated. Second, threat and anxiety are diminished, allowing students to function at high levels. And third, learning involves real or simulated "whole" experiences that tap into many ways of thinking, expressing, and doing. Teachers may use many effective brain-based strategies to deepen students' understanding. Figure 4.7 is adapted from the work of Eric Jensen (2000). Figure 4.8 connects some brain-framed activities to the thinking functions they support.

Materials/Resources

The variety of instructional materials available is extensive and at times overwhelming. Learning resources and materials must be appropriate to the needs and interests of the students. Sometimes the only materials needed are a pencil and paper (or word processor). Other times, more extensive resources are needed for exploration and research. Generally the teacher selects learning resources for young learners. But as students take more responsibility for their learning, they begin to search out information and learning resources on their own. Guidance and support at this stage helps students become independent learners and users of the vast number of resources at their disposal.

Some schools use a commercial textbook program as the required curriculum. When this is the case, state or district learning standards are used as a filter in selecting what is important to teach from the textbook. A comparison of learning standards and textbook objectives points out instructional priorities and enables the teacher to eliminate some textbook material. This standards-driven approach makes the curriculum more manageable.

Technology-related materials can support and enhance student learning. However, those that are technology based should be carefully chosen. Technology to support teaching the learning standards is the foremost consideration. Some technology-based applications can include the following:

- explore a concept using video discs, computer software programs, or the Internet
- present a concept or idea using video discs, computer software, or presentational tools (PowerPoint, HyperStudio)
- analyze and sort data and information using database programs
- create artistic products using graphic and sound design

Other resources for learning extend beyond the classroom into the community. Partnerships with governmental agencies, local businesses, and professional organizations can be a source of extended learning opportunities for students. Joining resources helps build greater understanding of the relationship between schooling and real-world applications.

---

7. Debate, Discuss, Debrief
Provide opportunities for students to explain their thinking in a nonthreatening environment. Communication is the key for deepening understanding.

8. Game Making
Use a known game genre into which the new concepts and material are incorporated.

9. Presentations
Provide opportunities for students to use technology or visual aids, or to process information and transform it for others.

Activities such as those described in this figure allow students to do something, to use concepts, ideas, strategies, and processes. This use and manipulation of material is the vehicle to deepen understanding by weaving it into existing knowledge.

Figure 4.7 (continued)

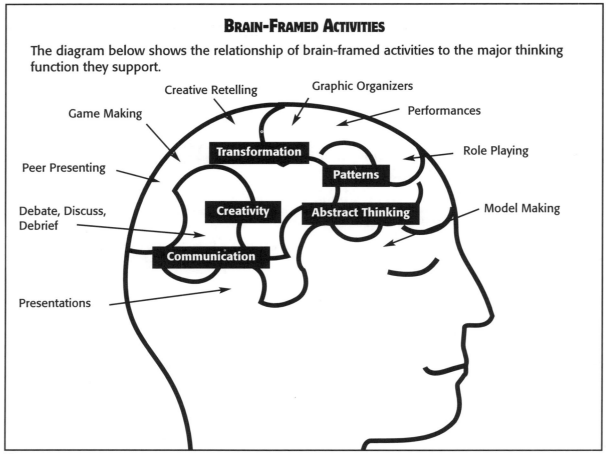

BRAIN-FRAMED ACTIVITIES

The diagram below shows the relationship of brain-framed activities to the major thinking function they support.

Creative Retelling

Graphic Organizers

Game Making

Performances

Peer Presenting

Transformation

Patterns

Role Playing

Debate, Discuss, Debrief

Creativity

Abstract Thinking

Model Making

Communication

Presentations

Figure 4.8

Grouping Pattern

The benefits of cooperative learning groups have been known for many years. Students in cooperative learning settings tend to perform better academically than students taught in individualistic or competitive settings (Johnson and Johnson 1984). Bellanca and Fogarty (1991) state: "Research on cooperative learning is overwhelmingly positive and the cooperative approaches are appropriate for all curriculum areas. The more complex the outcomes (high-order processing of information, problem solving, social skills and attitudes), the greater are the effects." There are times, however, when individual or whole group activities are appropriate. The key is to balance whole group teacher directed activities with cooperative learning groups (Zemelmann, Daniels, and Hyde 1993; Skowron 1990). Types of grouping arrangements in relation to instructional purposes are described in Figure 4.9.

GROUPING STUDENTS FOR INSTRUCTION

GROUPING ARRANGEMENT	DESCRIPTION	PURPOSE
WHOLE CLASS	Students participate as a whole class with the teacher in a directed instructional activity.	• presentation of information • demonstration/modeling of a process • outlining directions • sharing/reporting/communicating/presenting the work of cooperative groups
COOPERATIVE GROUPS	Students work with others in a cooperative group arrangement in which students are responsible for the group's activities. The teacher is a facilitator to the groups. Not all groups necessarily work on the same topic. A jigsaw approach specifies separate topics for each group with a whole class sharing at the conclusion of the project.	• solving a problem • exploring a topic • conducting an experiment • creating a model • developing a presentation • discussing concepts and ideas
INDEPENDENT WORK	The student focuses on a task to practice, reinforce, or extend specific learning or reflect on what he/she has learned. Independent work may be used when a student has missed some instruction or has not achieved the level of proficiency necessary. Independent work may also be appropriate when a student's capabilities show he/she would benefit from greater in-depth exploration of a topic.	• practicing skills (math, spelling) • reading (literature selection or content information) • summarizing/reflecting on personal learning • independent research
PAIR AND SHARE	Students find it beneficial to work with one other student when they need tutoring or reinforcement of a learning concept or skill. Pair and Share also provides an opportunity for students to discuss a topic of study or class event in terms of feelings and attitudes.	• reading each other's essays • listening to one another's stories • discussing what has been learned • discussing feelings and attitudes toward a given topic
SMALL GROUPS	Small group instruction is beneficial for teaching students who have common skill needs. The instruction is tailored to specifically meet the needs of the group. The groups are convened for a specific purpose and disbanded when the purpose is met.	• practicing letter/sound relationships • practicing correct use of the apostrophe in plural possessives • practicing fluency at the independent reading level • practicing the steps in using the calculator to perform specific operations • transposing music from key of C to key of F

Figure 4.9

Monitoring Student Progress

Monitoring students as they engage in a learning task is a crucial part of teaching. It is important for students to receive feedback on their progress throughout the learning activity. At times encouragement or positive affirmation is all that is needed. At other times clarification or instructional guidance is necessary to prevent misunderstandings. When confused, some students willingly ask for help. Other students do not. And still others do not even know they are confused. Monitoring all students is important to obtain diagnostic feedback and determine when intervention through reteaching or additional practice is necessary.

There are several ways to monitor students, ranging from observation in the classroom setting to performance tests and quizzes. Some general questions the teacher may use during monitoring are as follows:

Does the student exhibit confusion?

Is the student off task?

Has the student finished too soon or not soon enough?

Does the student understand the directions?

Is there some prior knowledge or prerequisite information the student needs?

Does the student's response indicate understanding?

A checklist may be used to monitor student progress during a learning activity. The checklist contains key criteria against which the students are observed (Burke 1994). A sample checklist for informational reading at the elementary level appears in Figure 4.10. The checklist will help determine which students have common difficulties. These students may then be grouped for reteaching, reinforcement, or practice activities.

Another form of student monitoring is through direct questioning on what is being learned. Questioning may be through a verbal exchange between teacher and student or in written form, through quizzes, summaries, or reflections. The type of monitoring a teacher chooses to do depends on the

GUIDEBOOK

OBSERVATION CHECKLIST: READING FOR INFORMATION

Name																	
Uses prediction																	
Visualization apparent through descriptive illustration																	
Understands descriptive text																	
Recalls sequence and order																	
Compares and contrasts ideas presented in text																	
Explains cause/effect relationships																	
States opinion and gives reasons																	
Connects sources of information																	
Links reading to prior knowledge																	
Uses inferential thinking																	
Self-corrects																	
Exhibits independence																	

3 = Needs further instruction
2 = Shows developing understanding
1 = Demonstrates understanding

Figure 4.10

demands of the learning situation and the level of complexity and difficulty of the learning standards. Generally, more complex learning is better monitored through observation and questioning. Literal learning is more easily monitored through written quizzes and tests.

Ending/Summary/Reflection

When one links new learning to prior knowledge, one's mental map of information, concepts, skills, processes, attitudes, values, and beliefs related to a topic is expanded. This mental map is the schema or linked collection of related thoughts and ideas and is the operating base within which new information is integrated. Schema is expanded and understanding deepened through metacognitive processing and reflection. Seifert (1999) states that reflection is the partner of experience. Reflection and experience lead us to construct meaning. It is therefore important that students have opportunities for metacognitive processing throughout and especially at the conclusion of a learning experience. Notebook journals, audio journals, and sketchpads are some means for students to reflect and record the impact of their learning and thinking.

Practice Activities/Assignments

Not all students progress at the same pace. Monitoring and observation will indicate which students need more instruction or practice. For these students, it is appropriate to provide additional activities to reinforce learning. Practice activities should be interesting, well designed, and assigned only as necessary.

Section 3: Evidence of Learning

The purpose of assessment is to determine what the student has learned in relation to the learning standard. Since assessment is aligned to a learning standard, classroom instruction likewise must be aligned to that standard. Alignment of learning standards, instructional activities, and the assessment ensures that students are assessed on what was taught. If the standard is to identify rocks and minerals by their appearance, then students are assessed as they look at rocks and minerals and tell what they are. The teaching/learning activities that occur prior to the assessment provide input and practice on the physical appearance of rocks and minerals and how to identify them. When this is the case, there is no need for additional "test prep." The learning activities themselves are the preparation—and in some cases, may even be the assessment.

Assessment Strategies

The learning standard is the basis for assessment. Assessment strategies are formulated in the initial stage of planning and reconsidered and finalized with the completed instructional plan (see Figure 4.11). The type of assessment selected will vary according to the type of learning that is expected.

In the broadest sense, assessments may be classified as selected response or performance based. Selected response assessments include the pencil-paper "traditional" forms of testing (i.e., true-false, multiple choice, short answer). These assessments are useful in determining the student's content knowledge related to facts, information, and processes. Performance-based assessments are those that allow students to demonstrate what they can do with the learning they have acquired. Performance-based assessments include writing an essay, conducting research, preparing a report, presenting a demonstration, singing, playing a musical instrument, and performing a physical activity.

Students want to know how they will be assessed and evaluated. Parents also want to know what their student is learning and how he or she is progressing. Assessment tools such as rubrics and checklists help students understand what is to be learned by pointing out criteria and performance levels. They also clearly convey information about expectations and progress to parents (Burke 1994). When students and parents know the criteria and expectations, student performance often improves.

MENTORING

PLANNING GUIDE–BASIC INSTRUCTION
SECTION 3: EVIDENCE OF LEARNING
Use these questions to plan a basic instructional design.

PLANNING QUESTIONS AND DECISIONS	INFORMATION AND DATA SOURCES	NOTES AND COMMENTS
1. How will students demonstrate their learning?	See curriculum resource information and best practices information related to types of assessment: criterion referenced assessment, performance assessment, observation, standardized.	
2. How will the assessment be scored?	Consider use of a rubric, template, or Scantron scoring.	
3. How will learning be reported?	Consider appropriate types of feedback to students, use of a grading scale, parent reports, report cards, portfolios, etc. If feasible, electronic data may also be useful.	Refer to your planning notes in section one as you finalize decisions regarding assessment.
4. How will the assessment results be used?		Use assessment results to determine student strengths and weaknesses and plan the next lessons.

Figure 4.11

(continued on next page)

SECTION 3: EVIDENCE OF LEARNING
Planing Questions and Decisions

1. How will students demonstrate their learning?
Science log entry of experiment—steps and conclusions
Forced choice test (20 items)
Present report to class

2. How will the assessment be scored?
Rubric
Answer key: (20 items, 5 points each). Sign up to use scantron for scoring.

3. How will learning be reported?
Copy of rubric showing performance level will be returned to students. Teacher comments will be included as appropriate.
Go over test items with students. Grades will be determined according to the school-wide grading scale.
Copy of rubric showing performance level will be returned to students. Teacher comments will be included as appropriate.

4. How will the assessment results be used?
Determine which students need additional practice. Include results in quarterly report card grade. Students make revisions as necessary.
Determine which students need reinforcement of factual information. Students make corrections as necessary. Include results in quarterly report card grade.
The rubric will provide feedback to the student. A total of 5 points will be included in the quarterly report card grade.

Figure 4.11 (continued)

Using the Basic Instructional Design Planning Guide

The Basic Instructional Design Planning Guide is a thinking process approach to instructional planning. Preservice and novice teachers will find it helpful to follow all the steps in the guide. Understanding the thinking process underlying instructional design makes subsequent planning easier and provides a foundation for planning more complex instruction. Below are suggestions for using the planning guide.

1. Read the planning guide in its entirety.

It is good practice to become thoroughly familiar with the planning guide before using it. Doing so saves time in the long run. Get the "big picture" in mind before filling in the details.

2. Think it through.

Begin with Section 1: Desired Results. Think about the questions in column one and write down your thoughts and reactions. Consult the data and information sources suggested in column two and note the reminders and supplemental information in column three. Add notes and comments for later reference. Continue through Section 2: Lesson Design and Section 3: Evidence of Learning.

3. Synthesize the information.

The thinking process in step two provides a great deal of information which now must be synthesized into a coherent plan for instruction. The Basic Lesson Plan Form (see Blackline 4.4) is a synthesis and summary of the decisions made in working through the Basic Instructional Design Planning Guide. It is an action plan and a presentational overview for classroom instruction. An example of how this guide has been used by a seventh-grade science teacher appears in Figure 4.12.

When a novice teacher uses the planning guide over and over, he or she becomes familiar and comfortable with the planning process. With experience the teacher is able to take shortcuts in planning by using the lesson plan form without filling out the planning guide. This shortcut is possible when the planning questions are practiced and well known.

LESSON PLAN – GRADE 7 SCIENCE

LEARNING STANDARDS/BENCHMARKS (concepts, skills, processes)
Students will differentiate mixtures that are solutions and those that are not.

LESSON DESIGN	MATERIALS/RESOURCES	STUDENT GROUPING ARRANGEMENT
Opening (outcomes/purpose/expectations) Describe problem scenario: A forensic scientist is working with a detective to solve a criminal case. Show two beakers. Ask: How can the scientist tell which beaker contains water and which contains a mixture of salt and water? Discuss responses. Record responses for later review. Ask: Why is it important to be able to identify substances?	Beakers/mixtures Chart paper, markers	Whole class
Teaching Strategies/Activities (demonstration, modeling, explanation, directions, etc.) Describe lab set up and activity. (Refer to Lab Activity manual.) Review lab safety. Distribute/review experiment procedure.		
Student Activities Complete lab activity. Record findings in lab manual.	Safety glasses, lab aprons, graduated cylinders, clear beakers, stirring rods, six prepared mixtures, testing substances as listed in activity manual.	Three students per group (prearranged by teacher) Lab manual entries—individual
Closing (connections/summary/reflection) Groups 1, 2, 3 to report findings. Compare results. Verbalize conclusions. Review opening activity discussion. Discuss what was learned in the lab activity. Record two or more important concepts from this experiment in lab manual.		Whole class Lab manual entry—individual
PRACTICE ACTIVITIES/ASSIGNMENTS View video disc segment on this experiment and record results in lab manual.		Individual or small group depending on who is absent. Arrange with resource center for viewing and completion of work.
MONITORING STUDENT PROGRESS (ongoing) Informal observation and coaching during group work.		
ASSESSMENT OF STUDENT LEARNING 1. In small groups, students will use the rubric to evaluate their lab manual entries. 2. Twenty item completion test on content.		**EXPECTATIONS** Students will meet or exceed all categories on rubric. Students will achieve 80% correct to meet expectations, 90% to exceed expectations.

Figure 4.12

Basic Instructional Design

REFERENCES

Bellanca, J., and R. Fogarty. 1991. *Blueprints for thinking in the cooperative classroom.* Arlington Heights, IL: SkyLight Training and Publishing, Inc.

Burke, K. 1994. *How to assess authentic learning.* Arlington Heights, IL: SkyLight Training and Publishing, Inc.

Cummings, C. 1980. *Teaching makes a difference.* Edmonds, WA: Teaching, Inc.

Danielson, C. 1996. *Enhancing professional practice: A framework for teaching.* Alexandria, VA: Association for Supervision and Curriculum Development.

Ellis, A. K., and J. T. Fouts. 1997. *Research on educational innovations.* Larchmont, NY: Eye on Education.

Fogarty, R. 1997. *Brain-compatible classrooms.* Arlington Heights, IL: SkyLight Training and Publishing.

Good, T., and J. Brophy. 1997. *Looking in classrooms.* New York: Addison Wesley Longman.

Hunter, M. 1984. Knowing, teaching, and supervising. In *Using what we know about teaching and learning,* edited P. Hosford, pp.169-192. Alexandria, VA: Association for Supervision and Curriculum Development.

Jensen, E. 2000. *Brain based learning.* Del Mar, CA: Turning Point Publishing.

Johnson, D., and R. Johnson. 1984. *Circles of Learning.* Alexandria, VA: Association for Supervision and Curriculum Development.

Seifert, K. L. 1999. *Reflective thinking and professional development.* Boston: Houghton Mifflin.

Skowron, J. 1990. Frameworks for reading instruction. *Illinois Reading Council Journal.* 18(1): 15-21.

Wiggins, G., and J. McTighe. 1998. *Understanding by design.* Alexandria, VA: Association for Supervision and Curriculum Development.

Zemelman, S., H. Daniels, and A. Hyde. 1993. *Best practice: New standards for teaching and learning in America's schools.* Portsmouth, NH: Heinemann.

Four Blackline masters are provided on the pages that follow:
- Planning Guide—Section 1: Desired Results
- Planning Guide—Section 2: Lesson Design
- Planning Guide—Section 3: Evidence of Learning
- Basic Lesson Plan Form

Mentors may use these guides as they coach mentees in how to plan basic lessons and choose appropriate teaching strategies, grouping plans, and assessments.

PLANNING GUIDE–BASIC INSTRUCTION
SECTION 1: DESIRED RESULTS
Use these questions to plan a basic instructional design.

PLANNING QUESTIONS AND DECISIONS	INFORMATION AND DATA SOURCES	NOTES AND COMMENTS
1. What learning standards/ benchmarks will be taught?		
2. What is the specific learning standard?		
3. What assessment activities will enable students to demonstrate they have met the learning standard?		
4. What performance expectations are there for students to show the extent of learning that has occurred?		
5. How will students' difficulties be recognized along the way?		
6. What assessment materials are available and what materials need to be developed?		
7. How will assessment results be communicated to students and parents?		

Blackline 4.1

PLANNING GUIDE—BASIC INSTRUCTION
SECTION 2: DESIGN
Use these questions to plan a basic instructional design.

PLANNING QUESTIONS AND DECISIONS	INFORMATION AND DATA SOURCES	NOTES AND COMMENTS
1. What are the learning standards/benchmarks to be achieved?		
2. What is a motivating opening for the lesson?		
3. What strategies or activities will be used to teach the standard?		
4. What materials are needed to support and enhance learning?		
5. What is the appropriate use of technology?		
6. How will students be grouped for this activity?		
7. What opportunities will students have to reflect on their learning?		
8. How will student progress be monitored?		
9. What forms of additional practice may be necessary?		
10. How long will the lesson take?		
11. Are there any foreseeable pitfalls in this lesson?		
12. What alternatives are there if the lesson doesn't work out?		

Blackline 4.2

PLANNING GUIDE—BASIC INSTRUCTION
SECTION 3: EVIDENCE OF LEARNING
Use these questions to plan a basic instructional design.

PLANNING QUESTIONS AND DECISIONS	INFORMATION AND DATA SOURCES	NOTES AND COMMENTS
1. How will students demonstrate their learning?		
2. How will the assessment be scored?		
3. How will learning be reported?		
4. How will the assessment results be used?		

Blackline 4.3

Basic Instructional Design

BASIC LESSON PLAN FORM

LEARNING STANDARDS/BENCHMARKS (concepts, skills, processes)

LESSON DESIGN Opening (outcomes/purpose/expectations)	MATERIALS/RESOURCES	STUDENT GROUPING ARRANGEMENT
Teaching Strategies/Activities (demonstration, modeling, explanation, directions, etc.)		
Student Activities		
Closing (connections/summary/reflection)		
PRACTICE ACTIVITIES/ASSIGNMENTS		
MONITORING STUDENT PROGRESS (ongoing)		
ASSESSMENT OF STUDENT LEARNING		EXPECTATIONS

Blackline 4.4

SkyLight Professional Development

In addition to designing a basic lesson plan, teachers can design a unit plan that addresses curriculum goals and standards and allows students to demonstrate their abilities through a variety of learning experiences and assessments. Mentors can guide protégés in the development of two- to three-week integrated units.

How Should We Use Multiple Intelligences?

by **Kay Burke**

Teachers are experimenting with a variety of instructional methods and assessments to evaluate students' achievement and progress toward meeting standards. Some educators are also experimenting with planning integrated instructional units that include learning experiences from all of the multiple intelligences. Using a graphic organizer such as the grid on Blackline 5.1 (at the end of this selection) to devise the unit plan helps groups of teachers focus on standards, integrate their curricula, brainstorm learning experiences and assessments, and decide on the key whole-class assessments to capture important concepts in the unit. This approach, as detailed below, helps teams of teachers or individual teachers plan a unit that synthesizes cooperative learning, higher-order thinking, portfolios, and performance tasks as well as rubrics with the multiple intelligences. (See Figure 5.1 for learning experiences and assessments classified by multiple intelligences.)

Adapted from *How to Assess Authentic Learning,* 3rd ed. by K. Burke, pp. 43–45, 47–50, 53. © 1999 by SkyLight Training and Publishing.

Thirteen Steps to Develop a Unit Plan

The following format for developing a unit plan can be adapted to meet the needs of the teacher or a group of teachers. (Sample unit plans appear in Figures 5.2, 5.3, and 5.4.)

1. Decide on a unit or theme that will last at least two to three weeks. The unit could be on a specific topic (Oceanography or Greek Mythology), a book (Stephen Crane's *The Red Badge of Courage*), or a country (Egypt). Some teachers choose to work on a thematic or integrated unit that connects several content areas. Some thematic units might include:

   - Health and Wellness
   - Justice in America
   - Off to Work We Go
   - Crime and Punishment
   - A Decade—The 1920s
   - The Future
   - Heroes

2. Draw a grid on large pieces of newsprint or use a blank grid.

3. Decide on the standards and/or benchmarks that will be the major goals of the unit. What should the students be able to do at the end of the unit?

4. Distribute sticky notes to each participant. Ask participants to brainstorm ideas for learning experiences or assessments for the unit and write one idea per sticky note. (See Figure 5.1 for ideas for learning experiences.) Allow five minutes for individual thinking and writing. Remember to be specific. Don't say "Read a book about oceans"—recommend *Chadwick the Crab*.

5. Read each idea and decide where it should go on the grid. Remember that many ideas cross over into other intelligences. For example, holding a mock trial to determine whether President Roosevelt suspected Pearl Harbor was going to be bombed could be

classified as interpersonal, bodily/kinesthetic, or verbal/linguistic. Just place the idea where you think it goes or where you need more selections.

6. Review the grid to make sure there are at least three learning experiences/assessments for each intelligence. Remember, many activities are assessments. For example, creating a Venn diagram to compare and contrast Hemingway and Faulkner is an activity; it is also an assessment.

7. Decide on four learning experiences from the grid that would benefit the whole class. Consider the following criteria for selecting each experience:

   - Does the experience help meet the standards?
   - Does it include several intelligences? (Does it meet the needs of more students?)
   - Is it worth the time to do it?
   - Can it be assessed?
   - Is it doable in my class? (time, resources, money, space)
   - Is it fun and motivating?
   - Will it meet the diverse needs of my students?

8. Write the four learning experiences in the boxes on the bottom of the grid. Remember that teachers on the team may select different whole-class experiences based upon their focus for the unit and the individual needs of their students.

9. Decide on how to assess the four learning experiences selected. Remember to combine traditional assessments (quizzes, tests, research reports) with performance assessments (logs, journals, portfolios, projects).

10. Create a culminating event to bring closure to the unit. The event should synthesize all the ideas and provide a showcase for the students to share their learnings with a wider audience. Examples of culminating events include mock trials, field trips, portfolio exhibitions, plays, costume days, medieval banquet, Renaissance fair, job fairs, and re-enactments.

11. Develop a portfolio that includes three to four teacher-selected items to show the students have met the standards. Allow students to select four or five other entries from the grid for their student choices.

12. Create rubrics to evaluate projects, group or individual performances, and the portfolio. Students can work in their groups to determine the criteria for each project. Teachers usually decide on four or five group projects and let students choose their groups. Groups could be divided as follows:

    - Research reports
    - Videotaped interviews
    - Simulations or performances
    - Newspaper stories
    - PowerPoint presentations

    Each group reviews samples of the product and determines the criteria that is necessary to create a successful product or performance. For example, the group creating the video could decide on three criteria regarding the sound element: loudness, dialogue clarity, and overall effect. They could then develop a rubric to help them prepare the video and to assess it for the final evaluation. The students and teacher may need to refine the rubric and add more focused descriptors as they work on the project, but it at least makes them aware of all the components they need to address.

13. Create a rubric to assess the portfolio. It could include criteria such as completeness, timeliness, understanding of content, visuals/graphics, reflections, mechanics, organization, etc. Many of the items included would have been graded previously; therefore, one grade using a weighted rubric could be used. The students should be a part of the discussion about criteria and should self-evaluate their own portfolio using the rubric.

Figure 5.1, on the following page, classifies learning experiences and assessments by multiple intelligences. Three samples of unit plans organized by multiple intelligences are also provided in Figures 5.2, 5.3, and 5.4.

REFERENCES

Gardner, H. 1983, 1993. *Frames of mind: The theory of multiple intelligences—Tenth anniversary edition.* NY: Basic Books.

A Blackline master is provided at the end of this selection. This blackline provides a planning guide for creating a unit of study. Protégés may use the blackline to plan their units. Mentors can help protégés design units by assisting them in filling out the blackline and suggesting activities and assessments for the multiple intelligences. Protégés can also work in teams to create units.

Learning Experiences

VERBAL/ LINGUISTIC
Speeches
Debates
Storytelling
Reports
Crosswords
Newspapers
Internet

LOGICAL/ MATHEMATICAL
Puzzles
Outlines
Timelines
Analogies
Patterns
Problem-solving
Lab experiments
Formulas

VISUAL/ SPATIAL
Artwork
Photographs
Math manipulatives
Graphic organizers
Posters, charts
Illustrations
Cartoons
Props for plays
Use of overhead

BODILY/ KINESTHETIC
Field trips
Role-playing
Learning centers
Labs
Sports/games
Cooperative learning
Body language
Experiments

MUSICAL/ RHYTHMIC
Background music
Songs about books,
people, countries,
historic events
Raps
Jingles
Choirs

INTERPERSONAL
Group video, film,
slides
Team computer
programs
Think-pair-share
Cooperative tasks
Jigsaws
Conferences

INTRAPERSONAL
Reflective journals
Learning logs
Goal-setting journals
Metacognitive
reflections
Independent
reading
Silent reflection
Diaries

NATURALIST
Outdoor education
Environmental
studies
Field trips (farm,
zoo)
Bird watching
Nature walk
Weather forecasting
Stargazing
Exploring nature
Ecology studies
Identifying leaves

Figure 5.1

SAMPLE

Oceanography Unit

Subject Area: *Integrated Unit—Elementary*   **Timeline:** *3–4 weeks*

Major Goals of Unit:

1. *Know the major difference between fresh and ocean water*
2. *Know that an organism's patterns of behavior are related to the nature of that organism's environment*
3. *Know that the transfer of energy (e.g., through the consumption of food) is essential to all living organisms*

List at least three learning experiences/assessments under each intelligence.

VERBAL/LINGUISTIC	LOGICAL/MATHEMATICAL	VISUAL/SPATIAL	BODILY/KINESTHETIC
• *Read* Chadwick the Crab. • *Read story* Curious Clownfish. • *Organize characters from* Curious Clownfish *in chronological order.* • *Read* Leroy the Lobster. • *Research the effects of oil slicks in the ocean and on marine life.*	• *Measure with yarn the length of the blue whale.* • *Research sizes of whales.* • *Measure and draw sizes of whales in chalk on the blacktop.* • *Estimate the number of shells in container.* • *Classify the types of shells.*	• *Create whale models to hang around the room.* • *Create a bulletin board about the ocean.* • *Create a mural of the ocean.* • *Make food-chain mobiles.* • *Make a model of your favorite ocean creature.* • *Draw a web that shows attributes of sea creatures.* • *Make a model of your favorite creature.*	• *Play crab soccer.* • *Listen to ocean music and create a clay model of what you feel.* • *Imitate the movements of an octopus, crab, fish, or sea anemone.*

MUSICAL/RHYTHMIC	INTERPERSONAL	INTRAPERSONAL	NATURALIST
• *Play ocean mood music (such as Free Willy music).* • *Listen to sounds of the ocean (whales, dolphins).* • *Design instruments to mimic water sounds.*	• *Choose an ocean animal to research and give an oral presentation with a partner.* • *In small groups, discuss products we receive from the ocean.* • *Interview students who have been to the ocean.* • *Do a KWL chart before you begin the unit.*	• *Pretend you are an ocean animal.* • *Write a story about your life (or a day) as an animal that lives in the ocean.* • *Reflect on how pollution affects you.* • *Write a reflective journal on the sounds of the ocean.*	• *Visit the aquarium.* • *Explore ocean-related careers.* • *Adopt an ocean animal.* • *Make predictions about ocean life.* • *Graph tides or water temperature.*

1. Whole-class learning experiences:	*Research report on an ocean animal*	*Oral presentation of report*	*Model of an ocean creature*	*Portfolio that contains 7 items*
2. Whole-class assessments for learning experiences:	*Checklist (point system)*	*Videotape for self-assessment*	*Criteria checklist*	*Rubric*
3. Culminating event for unit:	*Field trip to the local aquarium*			

Figure 5.2   Adapted from Training the Trainers workshop, Summer 1996, Chicago.

Greek Mythology

Subject Area: _Integrated Unit—Middle School_   **Timeline:** _4–6 weeks_

Major Goals of Unit:

1. _Communicate ideas in writing to describe, inform, persuade, and entertain_

2. _Demonstrate comprehension of a broad range of reading materials_

3. _Use reading, writing, listening, and speaking skills to research and apply information for specific purposes_

List at least three learning experiences/assessments under each intelligence.

VERBAL/LINGUISTIC	LOGICAL/MATHEMATICAL	VISUAL/SPATIAL	BODILY/KINESTHETIC
• Read The Iliad. • Read The Odyssey. • Read Edith Hamilton's Mythology. • Write an original myth to explain a scientific mystery. • Write poems about mythology. • Write a eulogy for a fallen Greek or Trojan warrior.	• Use a Venn diagram to compare the Greeks and the Trojans. • Create original story problems that can incorporate Pythagorean theorem. • Draw a family tree of the twelve Olympians and their children. • Complete a timeline of Odysseus' trip home from Troy.	• Draw the battle plan for the Greeks' attack on Troy. • Draw Mt. Olympus. • Sketch the Greek gods and goddesses. • Create a video of the Olympic games. • Draw items that relate to mythology.	• Act out a Greek tragedy. • Recreate some of the Olympic events. • Act out a myth. • Create a dance for the forest nymphs. • Reenact the battle scene between Hector and Achilles.

MUSICAL/RHYTHMIC	INTERPERSONAL	INTRAPERSONAL	NATURALIST
• Write a song for a lyre. • Pretend you are Apollo, God of Music, and CEO of Motown. • Select music that correlates with each god or goddess.	• Interview Helen about her role in the Trojan War. • Work in a group to create a computer crossword puzzle about mythology.	• Pretend you are a Greek soldier away from home for ten years. Keep a diary of your thoughts. • Write a journal about how you would feel if you were Prometheus chained to a rock. • Reflect on the effects of war on civilians.	• Using scientific data, predict how long it will take before anything grows after the Greeks destroy Troy and sow the fields with salt. • Describe the animals and plants on Mt. Olympus.

1. Whole-class learning experiences:

Read Hamilton's Mythology	Read excerpts from The Iliad and The Odyssey	Select a group project or performance	Portfolio that contains 7–10 items

2. Whole-class assessments for learning experiences:

Teacher-made test	Write a paper comparing the Greeks to the Trojans	Rubric to assess each one	Rubric created by class

3. Culminating event for unit:

Exhibition in the school gym—students and teachers dress up as favorite mythological characters. Invited guests view videos, portfolios, artifacts, and an original skit.

Figure 5.3

The Red Badge of Courage Unit

Subject Area: _American Literature—High School_   **Timeline:** _3 weeks_

Major Goals of Unit:
1. _Demonstrates competence in general skills and strategies for reading a variety of literary texts_
2. _Demonstrates competence in the general skills and strategies of the writing process_
3. _Demonstrates competence in speaking and listening as tools for learning_

List at least three learning experiences/assessments under each intelligence.

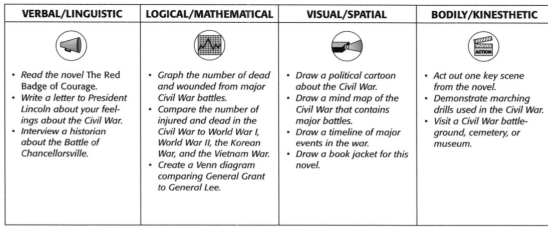

VERBAL/LINGUISTIC	LOGICAL/MATHEMATICAL	VISUAL/SPATIAL	BODILY/KINESTHETIC
• Read the novel The Red Badge of Courage. • Write a letter to President Lincoln about your feelings about the Civil War. • Interview a historian about the Battle of Chancellorsville.	• Graph the number of dead and wounded from major Civil War battles. • Compare the number of injured and dead in the Civil War to World War I, World War II, the Korean War, and the Vietnam War. • Create a Venn diagram comparing General Grant to General Lee.	• Draw a political cartoon about the Civil War. • Draw a mind map of the Civil War that contains major battles. • Draw a timeline of major events in the war. • Draw a book jacket for this novel.	• Act out one key scene from the novel. • Demonstrate marching drills used in the Civil War. • Visit a Civil War battleground, cemetery, or museum.

MUSICAL/RHYTHMIC	INTERPERSONAL	INTRAPERSONAL	NATURALIST
• Sing the songs the troops of the North and South sang while marching. • Learn the dances of the Civil War era. • Make up a ballad about Henry, the protagonist of the novel.	• Read other books about buddies during war time, such as All Quiet on the Western Front, Catch 22, and For Whom the Bell Tolls. • Write and act out a dialogue between two military buddies in either Vietnam, Korea, World War I, or World War II.	• Keep a daily diary of boot camp. • Write a poem about your feelings. • Write a last will and testament in case you die in battle. • Write a eulogy for a soldier who died in battle.	• Find specific passages where author Stephen Crane tells about how war destroys nature. • Write how the environment (weather, rivers, terrain) impacts battle decisions. • Research the effects weapons of destruction have on the environment.

1. Whole-class learning experiences:

Read the novel The Red Badge of Courage	Mind map on Civil War battles	Select one group project or performance	Portfolio that contains 7 items

2. Whole-class assessments for learning experiences:

Teacher-made test (numerical grade)	Checklist	Rubric to assess key criteria	Rubric to assess portfolio

3. Culminating event for unit:

Exhibition where students display artifacts they selected from the grid to include in their personal portfolios. Guests are invited to view videos, slides, and pictures from their projects.

Figure 5.4

How Should We Use Multiple Intelligences?

_____ **Unit**

Subject Area: _____   Timeline: _____

Major Goals of Unit: 1. _____

2. _____

3. _____

_____

List at least three learning experiences/assessments under each intelligence.

VERBAL/LINGUISTIC	LOGICAL/MATHEMATICAL	VISUAL/SPATIAL	BODILY/KINESTHETIC

MUSICAL/RHYTHMIC	INTERPERSONAL	INTRAPERSONAL	NATURALIST

1. Whole-class learning experiences:

2. Whole-class assessments for learning experiences:

3. Culminating event for unit:

Once instructional planning is in progress or completed, beginning teachers must also establish a classroom environment that is conducive for learning. Mentors should help the new teacher create procedures, rules, and consequences that provide clear expectations for student behavior.

Setting the Climate

by **Kay Burke**

Classroom Climate

> Improved school climate is an ideal, a goal to pursue. A school that claims that it has a perfect school climate is myopic, for improved school climate is something that professional educators are working toward—always (Hansen and Childs 1998, p. 14).

The climate of a classroom refers to the type of environment students are exposed to when they are learning. A person can get a feel for a school by walking in the halls, getting a view of the surroundings, and seeing how people treat one another. The climate of a school is often difficult to define, but it has a tremendous influence on learning.

Freiberg (1998) believes that school climate is an ever-changing factor in the lives of the students and teachers in a school, and states that "much like the air we breathe, school climate is ignored until it becomes foul" (p. 22). The school climate can either enhance learning or serve as a barrier to learning. Schools that have mandatory attendance at all school functions, lack of choice in curriculum, heavy emphasis on high-stakes testing and evaluation, and a litany of "not" rules ("students shall not chew gum") created and enforced by the faculty and staff isolate and separate the faculty from the students. Darling-Hammond (as cited in Hansen and Childs 1998) affirms that

Adapted from *What to Do with the Kid Who....* by K. Burke, pp. 67–88. © 2000 by SkyLight Training and Publishing.

"schools really are much alike, regardless of where they are. Mandates and regulations govern many school systems in ways that make schools impersonal, indifferent, and generally insensitive to the individuals within them" (p. 14).

In describing the climate of a classroom, educators should begin with a vision of what the classroom ought to be like. Kohn talks about the idea of climate as "one that promotes deep understanding, excitement about learning, and social as well as intellectual growth" (1996, p. 54). Kohn believes students need to play an active role in the decision-making process, teachers need to work with students to structure the curriculum to meet their needs and interests, and the environment needs to support children's desires to discover new ideas and their love of learning. A classroom where the teacher depends upon compliance from the students and uses a lock-step system of rewards and punishment to ensure their compliance does not foster an environment conducive to learning. Students need to construct knowledge for themselves and feel empowered to help make some decisions about their classroom environment and their own learning.

Classroom Management

Freiberg (1999) discusses the role Behaviorist Learning Theory has played in classroom management. He says that the most common approach to classroom management in many schools is some form of behavior modification. The key ingredients of most teachers' discipline routines include "rules, consequences, and rewards" that have their roots in classical conditioning theory derived by Pavlov and operant conditioning described by B. F. Skinner. Operant conditioning is the reinforcement of behavior (candy, tokens, stars) and its relationship to specific consequences. This conditioning takes place when teachers try to stop a particular response by the student with a specific action. Teachers engaging in this conditioning use a contingency plan or action that is repeated to reinforce or shape a particular response by the student. However, it has been found that not all psychological lessons learned with rats and pigeons in the laboratory translate well to the classroom.

Freiberg says that even though Cognitive Learning Theory, which focused on why people behave and think in certain ways, began to replace Behaviorist Learning Theory in the 1970s, behaviorism began to flourish in the American classroom in the 1960s and '70s. Commercial programs such as Assertive Discipline focused on controlling student behaviors by using punishments (name on the board, removal of privileges) and rewards (stars, tokens, extra recess). In one study, researchers Emmer and Aussiker (as cited in Freiberg 1999) demonstrated that student attitude toward school was lower in the Assertive Discipline school. Freiberg concluded that, "Discipline programs that are highly behavioristic and focus on controlling student behaviors through punishment can diminish student self-discipline" (p. 8).

On the other hand, school programs that emphasize student self-discipline (the responsibility model), rather than external controlling factors (the obedience model) (see Figure 6.1), show greater promise in improving achievement and learning environments (Gottfredson, Gottfredson, and Hybl as cited in Freiberg 1999). Schools that improve the academic achievements of their students not only emphasize academics, but also emphasize an open environment and a healthy school climate (Hoy, Tarter, and Kottkamp as cited in Freiberg 1999).

Obedience Model vs. Responsibility Model

- External control
- Internal control

- Fear of getting caught
- Desire to do the right thing

- Authority figures
- Self-discipline

Figure 6.1

Setting the Climate

Person-Centered Classrooms

Freiberg (1999) advocates a person-centered classroom management program that emphasizes caring, guidance, cooperation, and the building of self-discipline. Person-centered classrooms encourage students to think for themselves and to help each other. Emphasis is also placed on self-discipline that is built over time and encompasses many different experiences: "It requires a learning environment that nurtures opportunities to learn from one's own experiences, including mistakes, and to reflect on these experiences" (Freiberg 1999, p. 13). Figure 6.2 shows how the traditional "Teacher-Centered Classroom" differs from the "Person-Centered Classroom."

In the person-centered classroom, students self-regulate their learning and construct meaning for themselves. They initiate their learning, collaborate effectively with their peers, and self-evaluate their progress toward meeting their academic goals. They become prepared to function in a community of learners. Brophy (1999) believes teachers need to design their instructional and management methods to support this goal. This goal contrasts to the goal of the behaviorist model, which is to control students' behavior. As Brophy states: "Traditionally emphasized behavioristic management models, especially those designed to train students to follow unvaried routines and respond 'mindlessly' to cues, are not well suited to preparing them to fulfill today's more demanding roles" (p. 55).

A positive school and classroom climate is critical for learning. All the procedures, rules, consequences, metal detectors, and police support available cannot compensate for the absence of a school climate or culture that influences everything that goes on in a school. Peterson and Deal (1998) talk about how culture is the underground stream of norms, values, beliefs, traditions, and rituals that have built up out of time. They state: "This set of informal expectations and values shapes how people think, feel, and act in schools. This highly enduring web of influence binds the school together and makes it special. It is up to school leaders—principals, teachers, and often parents—to help identify, shape, and maintain strong, positive, student-focused cultures. Without these

Teacher-Centered Classrooms Compared to Person-Centered Classrooms

TEACHER-CENTERED CLASSROOMS	PERSON-CENTERED CLASSROOMS
The teacher is the sole leader.	Leadership is shared.
Management is a form of oversight.	Management is a form of guidance.
Teacher takes responsibility for all the paper-work and organization.	Students are facilitators for the operations of the classroom.
Discipline comes from the teacher.	Discipline comes from the self.
A few students are the teacher's helpers.	All students have the opportunity to become an integral part of the management of the classroom.
Teacher makes the rules and posts them for the students.	Rules are developed by the teacher and students in the form of a classroom constitution or compact.
Consequences are fixed for all students.	Consequences reflect individual differences.
Rewards are mostly extrinsic.	Rewards are mostly intrinsic.
Students are allowed limited responsibilities.	Students share in classroom responsibilities.
Few members of the community enter the classroom.	Partnerships are formed with business and community groups to enrich and broaden the learning opportunities for students.

(Adapted from Rogers and Freiberg 1994, p. 240.)
Reprinted with permission of Prentice Hall, Upper Saddle River, NJ.

Figure 6.2

Setting the Climate

supportive cultures, reforms will falter, staff morale and commitment will wither, and student learning will slip" (p. 28).

This selection explores ways in which teachers can create person-centered classrooms where students are involved in the decision-making process and encouraged to self-evaluate their behavior. By allowing students to make choices and by encouraging self-discipline, schools can create responsible, confident learners. Scenarios are presented throughout that represent ways teachers might facilitate implementation of classroom procedures with their students. Each scenario is followed by strategies, activities, and assignments to help teachers tackle the particular classroom issue outlined in the scenario.

Getting Started

"I feel it is very important that we always walk in the halls and enter the room slowly. Why do you think that procedure is important?" asks Mrs. Saunders.

"I saw a boy get hurt once when another boy was rushing into the room and knocked him into the doorknob," Mary replies.

"I don't like getting shoved by someone who is afraid of being late," adds John.

"So, you think we should all be courteous and enter the room walking rather than running or shoving?" Mrs. Saunders asks.

"Yes," says the class.

"All right, let's practice how we should all enter the room. Everyone file out quietly and stand by the drinking fountain down the hall. When I give the signal, you will all walk toward our classroom and enter the room the way we discussed."

[Students rehearse entering the classroom.]

"I really liked the way you took turns entering the room and going to your desks. Now, what do you think would be a consequence if someone forgot our procedure and ran into someone while running into the room?"

"I think that person should have to go back and practice walking into the room again," says Juan.

"He should also have to apologize to whoever he ran into 'cause no one likes to be pushed," Jack adds.

"Okay," says Mrs. Saunders, "I think we all agree on the importance of this procedure. We'll add this to our list of classroom procedures and consequences."

Setting Up the Classroom

Very few students function well in a chaotic environment. Even though students may pretend to enjoy having the freedom to do whatever they want, whenever they want, most of them prefer structures or routines so they know exactly what they are supposed to do. Structure can be implemented through the arrangement of the classroom, as well as through classroom procedures.

Room Arrangement

Before students walk into class on the first day of school, teachers should arrange the classroom to permit orderly movement, make efficient use of the available space, and keep potential disruptions to a minimum. This provides not only the students but also the teacher with an efficient and well-organized area in which to learn. Evertson, Emmer, Clements, and Worsham (1997) suggest that teachers consider the following four guidelines:

1. Keep high-traffic areas free of congestion.
2. Be sure all students can be easily seen by the teacher.
3. Keep frequently used materials and teaching supplies readily accessible.
4. Be certain students can easily see whole-class presentations and displays.

Figure 6.3 shows one possible configuration of a room in which students sit in cooperative groups and everyone has a clear view of the teacher, blackboard, and screen.

Possible Room Arrangement

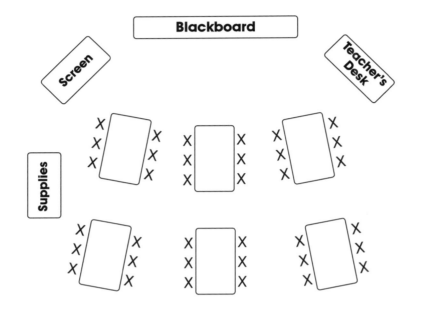

Figure 6.3

Procedures

Teachers can be creative and organize open-ended cooperative activities that allow students many options and choices while still providing them with structure. However, students need to walk before they can run, and it is essential that they know their boundaries the first week of class. Teachers should prepare a tentative list of procedures necessary for establishing the routines essential for classroom organization; however, the entire class should discuss the rationale for the procedures and have some input in their final adoption.

The most effective way for teachers to handle discipline problems is to prevent them. The proactive teacher anticipates potential management problems and establishes a positive classroom environment where students feel secure because they know what is expected of them. Researchers who have studied classroom management offer teachers the following tips:

- Proactive teachers help prevent discipline problems.
- Students who are actively involved in the lessons cause fewer behavior problems.
- Teachers who use instructional time efficiently have fewer management problems.

Good classroom management is primarily prevention, not intervention, planning before the year begins, implementing on the first day of school, and maintaining consistently throughout the year. "Procedures are ways of getting class activities done. Their function is to routinize tasks for continuity, predictability, and time saving" (Evertson and Harris 1991, p. 2). Evertson and Harris recommend four steps in teaching classroom procedures:

1. Explain:
   - Give concrete definition of procedures.
   - Provide the reason or rationale.
   - Demonstrate the procedure.
   - Present the task step by step.
   - Explain and demonstrate cues.
2. Rehearse the procedure.
3. Provide feedback to individuals and the class.
4. Re-teach procedures as necessary. (1991, p. 2)

The procedures in a class should relate to the important principles that permeate the classroom climate. If students are expected to be prepared, on time, courteous, and respectful of others' rights, the procedures should support those principles. Courteous and responsible behavior builds cooperation and teamwork. When this behavior is the standard, students feel obliged to treat other students the way they would like to be treated.

Teachers need to decide on the types of procedures that are needed for their students and be prepared to discuss the procedures during the first few days of school. Some procedures may be negotiable, and some procedures will be nonnegotiable.

Some of the procedures may have consequences if they are violated (see the Consequences section later in this selection). The teacher and the students should discuss the necessity of the procedures offered by the teacher, vote on their adoption, and post them in the room.

Many of the procedures should be rehearsed or role-played, and the teacher should gently remind students of the procedures by standing close to the student who is violating the procedure and pointing to the list of procedures posted in the room.

The key to effective procedures is consistency. If a procedure isn't working, it should be discussed and changed. But if the procedure is necessary and it is on the list, it should be enforced. A breakdown in classroom management doesn't usually start with a bang—it starts with a whimper!

Teachers can use Figure 6.4 to discern which procedures are important to implement in their classrooms. Teachers can prepare their own procedures with Blackline 6.1 provided at the end of this selection.

Classroom Procedures—
Do Students Know What Is Expected of Them for Routine Operations?

Directions: Review the following procedures and check the ones your students will need to know and practice.

A. Beginning the class

❏ How should students enter the room?

❏ What constitutes being late? (in the room, in the seat)

❏ How and when will absentee slips be handled?

❏ What type of seating arrangements will be used? (assigned seats, open seating, cooperative group seating)

❏ How will the teacher get students' attention to start class? (the tardy bell, a signal such as a raised hand, or lights turned off and on)

❏ How will students behave during Public Address (PA) announcements?

❏ Others:

_____

_____

_____

_____

_____

B. Classroom Management

❏ How and when will students leave their seats?

❏ What do students need in order to leave the room? (individual passes, room pass, teacher's permission)

❏ How will students get help from the teacher? (raise hands, put name on board, ask other group members first)

❏ What are acceptable noise levels for discussion, group work, seat work?

❏ How should students work with other students or move into cooperative groups? (moving desks, changing seats, noise level, handling materials)

❏ How will students get recognized to talk? (raised hand, teacher calls on student, talk out)

❏ How do students behave during presentations by other students?

❏ How do students get supplies?

❏ How and when do students sharpen pencils?

❏ How will students get materials or use special equipment?

❏ Others:

_____

_____

_____

_____

_____

Figure 6.4

(continued on next page)

C. Paperwork
- ❏ How will students turn in work? (put in specific tray or box, pass to the front, one student collects)
- ❏ How will students turn in makeup work if they were absent? (special tray, give to teacher, put in folder, give to teacher's aide)
- ❏ How will students distribute handouts? (first person in row, a group member gets a copy for all group members, students pick up as they enter room)
- ❏ How will late work be graded? (no penalty, minus points, zero, "F", use lunch or recess to finish, turn in by end of day, drop so many homework grades)
- ❏ How and when will students make up quizzes and tests missed? (same day they return to school, within twenty-four hours, within the week, before school, during lunch or recess, after school)
- ❏ How will late projects such as research papers, portfolios, and artwork be graded? (no penalty, minus points, lowered letter grade, no late work accepted)
- ❏ Others:

_____
_____
_____
_____
_____

D. Dismissal from Class or School
- ❏ How are students dismissed for lunch?
- ❏ When do students leave class for the day? (when bell rings, when teacher gives the signal)
- ❏ Can students stay after class to finish assignments, projects, tests?
- ❏ Can the teacher keep one student or the whole class after class or school?
- ❏ What do students do during fire and disaster drills?
- ❏ Others:

_____
_____
_____
_____
_____

E. Syllabus or Course Outline
- ❏ How are students made aware of course objectives?
- ❏ How are students made aware of course requirements?
- ❏ Are students given due dates for major assignments several weeks in advance?
- ❏ Are students told how they will be evaluated and given the grading scale?
- ❏ Others:

_____
_____
_____
_____
_____

Figure 6.4 (continued)

(continued on next page)

F. Other Procedures

You may need to introduce procedures related to recess, assemblies, guest speakers, substitute teachers, field trips, fire drills, teacher leaving the room, etc. List other procedures that are needed.

❏ _____
❏ _____
❏ _____

Recess

❏ _____
❏ _____
❏ _____
❏ _____

Assemblies

❏ _____
❏ _____
❏ _____
❏ _____

Guest Speakers

❏ _____
❏ _____
❏ _____
❏ _____

Substitute Teachers

❏ _____
❏ _____
❏ _____
❏ _____

Field Trips

❏ _____
❏ _____
❏ _____
❏ _____

Fire Drills

❏ _____
❏ _____
❏ _____
❏ _____

Figure 6.4 (continued)

Setting the Climate

Who Makes the Rules?

"Okay class," begins Mrs. Baker. "One of the rules on our web is 'Students should raise their hands to speak!' Let's talk about that rule before we vote on it."

"I don't like that rule," Mary offers. "When I get an idea, I have to blurt it out quickly or I'll lose it."

"Yeah," Sam agrees. "I hate holding my hand up."

"All right, Mary and Sam have some legitimate concerns about the rule. Let's role-play a situation and get a handle on this problem. I'll start talking about the Middle Ages, and we'll allow students to talk without raising their hands.

"One of the major problems confronting the people in the Middle Ages was the Bubonic Plague. Researchers estimate that as many as one-third of the population of Europe died because of the plague. One interesting thing about . . ."

"Is that like AIDS today?" Jimmy interrupts.

"Didn't rats spread the plague?" wonders Susan.

"Oh yuck, I hate rats!" shouts Juanita.

"Hey, my sister has a pet rat!" Susan cries.

"My next-door neighbor has a pet snake. I bet it eats rats!" yells Jimmy.

Finally, Mrs. Baker says, "Let's see. Yes, Jimmy, we are going to talk about how the plague compares to AIDS, and yes, Susan, the plague was spread by fleas on rats. We'll be talking about that more tomorrow. Let's see, what else?"

"Stop!" yells Mary. "I understand why we need to raise our hands to speak. When people blurt things out, we get off track. Also, it's rude to interrupt the teacher."

"I'm glad you can see how easy it is to get off track when somebody talks in the middle of my idea," says Mrs. Baker.

"I agree," Sam says. "I don't like people interrupting me. You need to finish your idea and then call on someone. I'll vote for it!"

"Let's take a vote. All those in favor of passing the rule to raise our hands to get recognized before we speak, please raise your hand!" says Mrs. Baker. "Great, 32 in favor; 3 opposed. We hereby pass Rule #1."

Discussing Classroom Rules

If classroom procedures form the framework for a classroom climate conducive to students and teachers working together cooperatively, the classroom rules form the heart and soul of caring, cooperative classrooms. If students are going to buy into the system, they must be part of the rule-making process. Classroom rules that are fair, reasonable, and enforceable play an important role in creating and maintaining a positive learning environment.

Terminology

Jones and Jones (1998) have some concerns about using the term *rules*. They believe the term suggests compliance to classroom management. Therefore, they suggest instead using terms such as *behavioral standards, norms, expectations, or principles* to "describe the agreements teachers and students make regarding the types of behaviors that help a classroom be a safe community of support" (p. 241).

Guidelines

According to Kohn (1991), "an immense body of research has shown that children are more likely to follow a rule if its rationale has been explained to them . . . Discipline based on reason is more effective than the totalitarian approach captured by the T-shirt slogan 'Because I'm the Mommy, that's why'" (p. 502).

Curwin and Mendler (1988) feel that effective rules describe specific behavior. They also believe that effective rules should be built on characteristics such as honesty, courtesy, helpfulness, and the like. Evertson and Harris (1991) offer eight guidelines for writing classroom rules.

Rules should be . . .

1. Consistent with school rules
2. Understandable
3. Doable (students able to comply)
4. Manageable

5. Always applicable (consistent)
6. Stated positively
7. Stated behaviorally
8. Consistent with teacher's own philosophy of how students learn best (p. 2)

Clearly stated rules that describe specific behavior enable students to understand what is expected of them. However, if rules are too specific, too many rules are needed. For example:

Too general: "Students shouldn't bother other students."

Too specific: "Students should not grab, push, shove, or trip other students."

Better rule: "It is best that students keep their hands off other people."

Other rules that could be developed include:

1. Respect other people's property.
2. Listen and be polite to other people.
3. Raise your hand to be recognized.
4. Obey all school rules.
5. Bring all materials to class.

A set of five rules should be sufficient to cover most classroom behaviors, but teachers sometimes may need to add a new rule to cover a situation not mentioned in the rules.

It is imperative that students get an opportunity to discuss the proposed classroom rules and understand the rationale behind the rules. A class meeting is the perfect opportunity to have a frank discussion of the rules, role-play situations, and come to a class consensus about the rules the students and teacher will adopt to ensure a positive and organized classroom environment.

It is important to note that some rules are nonnegotiable. Students must understand that the school district or the school sets down some rules that are not subject to a vote. Rules related to fighting, damage to property, injury to self or others, and weapons are absolute because they set parameters for all students to ensure their health and safety. It is important that teachers review school rules and the discipline policies with all students the first day of class.

After class members and the teacher have come to a consensus on their classroom rules, they should discuss and agree on the logical consequences students will face if they violate the rules. The old-fashioned punishment paradigm of teachers dictating all the rules and threatening students with punishments is not effective. As Kohn (1991) states, "reliance on the threat of punishment is a reasonably good indication that something is wrong in a classroom, since children have to be bullied into acting the way the teacher demands" (p. 500). Student ownership of the classroom encourages students to become stakeholders in the democratic process.

Consequences

If teachers are to establish an atmosphere of cooperation where students assume responsibility for their actions, the old obedience model of "spare the rod, spoil the child" is ineffectual. Kohn (1991) notes that "isolating a child from his peers, humiliating her, giving him an F, loading her with extra homework, or even threatening to do any of these things can produce compliance in the short run. Over the long run, however, this strategy is unproductive" (p. 500).

Many educators, however, feel that the role of consequences in breaking a rule is controversial. Even though many researchers feel that consequences are not punishment, Kohn (1996) calls them "Punishment Lite." He contends that the line between punishment and logical consequences is thin at times and even though the students have a "pseudochoice," as Kohn calls it, they are still being punished. Some discipline programs describe logical consequences as punitive revenge on students. If a student bites other students, he has to wear a sign saying "I bite people." If a student writes notes, she has to read them in front of the class. If a student misbehaves, he cannot go to lunch or the library or he must write an essay in the principal's office. If a student talks, he must stand in the corner and miss recess. If a student talks back to the teacher, she must write "I will not talk back to my teacher," 500 times.

Consequences, however, should relate directly to the rule violation and seem more logical than just punishments. Curwin and Mendler (1988) warn, however, that "a consequence can become a punishment if it is delivered aggressively" (p. 65). According to Curwin and Mendler consequences work best when they:

1. Are clear and specific
2. Have a range of alternatives
   - Reminder
   - Warning [or second reminder]
   - Conference with student
   - Conference with parent and/or administrator
3. Are not punishments
4. Are natural and/or logical
5. Are related to the rule

For example, if a student violates the rule about homework by not completing it, the consequence would not logically be to send that student to the principal. The consequence would more logically involve having the student turn in the homework before the end of the day, stay in from recess or lunch to finish it, or lose points. Consequences relate directly to the rule violation. Across-the-board punishments such as "sit in the corner," "go to the office," or "miss the field trip" are punitive and don't necessarily "fit the crime."

In addition, punishment often diminishes the dignity of the student as well as breeds resentment and resistance. Kohn (1991) says that punishment teaches nothing about what a student is supposed to do—only about what he or she is not supposed to do. Curwin and Mendler (1988) feel that if students are only motivated by a reward-and-punishment system, they will only behave out of fear of getting caught rather than out of a sense of social responsibility. And Glasser (1990) warns that students will not be coerced into doing anything. Students must see the rationale behind the rules and they must be a part of the process.

Some effective generic consequences include those outlined in Figure 6.5.

Offenses and Consequences

First offense   —   Reminder (many students simply forget the rule)

Second offense   —   Second reminder

Third offense   —   Conference with student

Fourth offense   —   Social contract with student

Fifth offense   —   Conference with parent and administrators

Figure 6.5

Other consequences should be specifically related to the rule (see Figure 6.6).

Examples

Rule
Students will be in their seats when the bell rings.

Consequences
1. Reminder
2. Second reminder
3. Student must make up time after school
4. Conference with student
5. Social contract
6. Conference with parent

Rule
Students will hand in homework on day it is due.

Consequences
1. Reminder
2. Conference with student
3. Student must stay in from recess or after school to complete homework
4. Points subtracted from grade
5. Conference with parent
6. Conference with counselor or administrator

Figure 6.6

If students have some input in the establishment of consequences, they are more likely to recognize fairness and logic in their implementation. Furthermore, teachers need to administer the consequences calmly and fairly and remind students that they still like and respect them—it is their actions that are unacceptable. Students who accept their consequences, realizing they have not fulfilled their responsibility or obligation, are likely to learn from their mistakes as long as they are treated with respect, confidentiality, and caring.

Blackline 6.2, at the end of this selection, contains Evertson's and Harris's (1991) criteria for creating effective classroom rules as well as a series of rules that may or may not meet their criteria. Blackline 6.3, at the end of this selection, that asks teachers to create five age-appropriate rules and the logical consequences that could be administered if students violate the rules.

Behavior Checklists

Hopefully, most students will accept the rule and consequence paradigm, internalize their own responsibilities, and model the positive behavior of their peers and teachers. The need still exists, however, for teachers to chronicle the behavior of those who choose not to cooperate. It is imperative that the documentation of all violations remains private and confidential.

Teachers can use a grade book, checklists, or any type of written format to monitor disruptive behavior. However, writing the names of misbehaving students on the blackboard and adding checks after their names for repeat offenses is not conducive to establishing classroom trust, nor does it build the self-esteem of students.

No teacher wants to take time away from teaching to be an accountant whose job is to debit and credit discipline violations, but there are ways teachers can monitor student behavior efficiently. A checklist may help teachers keep track of violations without embarrassing students or losing instructional time. It is suggested that teachers record specific dates under each rule violation to determine which consequence applies and to document persistent discipline problems in case more formal referrals or follow-up actions are required later. A behavior checklist (Blackline 6.4) is provided at the end of this selection.

Attitude Versus Skill Issue

Regardless of the terms or methods used to handle violations of rules, teachers sometimes tend to respond to student disruptions in a punitive way rather than trying to reinforce and redirect students to the correct behavior. Jones and Jones (1998) feel that school personnel have too often viewed inappropriate behavior as an attitude rather than a skill issue. In many cases, they assume the student's error is premeditated, deliberate, and threatening, when in fact, the student could be unaware of the violation, the disruption was accidental, or the student didn't know the skill. Social skills and behavior norms need to be taught and reinforced as much as math skills. Good behavior just doesn't happen—it has to be taught and reinforced. Figure 6.7 is an example of a brainstorming web teachers can use to get the class thinking about the rules needed. A Blackline master (Blackline 6.5) is provided at the end of this selection.

Brainstorming Web

Example: This web graphic organizer shows areas where rules may be needed.

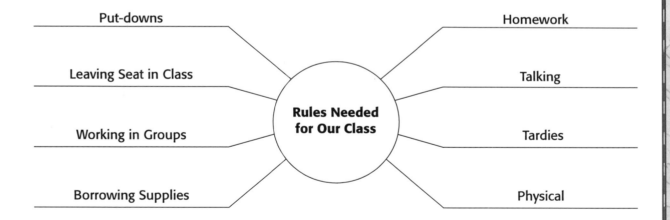

Figure 6.7

REFERENCES

Brophy, J. 1999. Perspectives of classroom management: Yesterday, today and tomorrow. In *Beyond behaviorism: Changing the classroom management paradigm*, edited by H.J. Freiberg. Boston: Allyn & Bacon

Evertson, C. M., Emmer, E. T., Clements, B. S., and Worsham, M. E. 1997. *Classroom management for elementary teachers*, 4th ed. Boston: Allyn & Bacon

Evertson, C., and Harris, A. 1991b. *Components of effective classroom management: Materials selected from the NDN-approved classroom organization and management program (COMP)*. Nashville, TN: Vanderbilt University.

Freiberg, H. J. 1998. Measuring school climate: Let me count the ways. *Educational Leadership* 56(1): 22–26.

Freiberg, H. J., ed. 1999. *Beyond behaviorism: Changing the classroom management paradigm*. Boston: Allyn & Bacon.

Glasser, W. 1990. *The quality school*. New York: Harper Perennial.

Hansen, J. M. and Childs, J. 1998. Creating a school where people like to be. *Educational Leadership* 56(1): 14–17.

Jones, V. F., and Jones, L. S. 1998. *Comprehensive classroom management: Creating communities of support and solving problems*, 5th ed. Boston: Allyn & Bacon.

Kohn, A. 1991. Caring kids: The role of the schools. *Phi Delta Kappan* 72(7): 496–506.

Kohn, A. 1996. *Beyond discipline: From compliance to community*. Alexandria, VA: Association for Supervision and Curriculum Development.

Peterson, K. D., and Deal, T. E. 1998. How leaders influence the culture of schools. *Educational Leadership* 56(1): 28–30.

Rogers, C., and Freiberg, H. J. 1994. *Freedom to Learn*, 3rd ed. Upper Saddle River, NJ: Prentice-Hall.

Five Blackline masters are provided in the pages that follow:
- Classroom Procedures Form
- Creating Effective Rules
- Classroom Rules and Consequences
- Behavior Checklist
- Brainstorming Web

Teachers can use all five to set up procedures and rules for their classrooms. Mentors can help mentees complete the Blacklines and choose procedures and rules that promote a positive classroom climate.

Classroom Procedures Form

Directions: Write the specific procedures you will implement with your students.

Teacher:_____ **Grade Level:**_____ **Class:**_____

A. Beginning the Class

❑ _____

❑ _____

❑ _____

❑ _____

❑ _____

❑ _____

B. Classroom Management

❑ _____

❑ _____

❑ _____

❑ _____

❑ _____

❑ _____

C. Paperwork

❑ _____

❑ _____

❑ _____

❑ _____

❑ _____

❑ _____

(continued on next page)

Blackline 6.1

D. Dismissal from Class or School

❏ _____
❏ _____
❏ _____
❏ _____
❏ _____
❏ _____

E. Syllabus or Course Outline

❏ _____
❏ _____
❏ _____
❏ _____
❏ _____
❏ _____

F. Bringing Books, Notebooks, and Supplies to Class

❏ _____
❏ _____
❏ _____
❏ _____
❏ _____
❏ _____

G. Other Procedures

❏ _____
❏ _____
❏ _____
❏ _____
❏ _____
❏ _____

(continued on next page)

Blackline 6.1 (continued)

Creating Effective Rules

Guidelines for effective rules (Evertson and Harris 1996, p. 2):

1. Consistent with school rules
2. Understandable
3. Doable (students able to comply)
4. Manageable

5. Consistent
6. Stated positively
7. Stated behaviorally
8. Consistent with teacher's own philosophy of how student's learn best

Directions: Review the following guidelines and then check to see if the seven rules meet the above criteria for classroom rules. If so, mark the rule "Yes." If not, mark it "No" and rewrite the rule to make it a "Yes."

Rules	YES	NO

1. Don't talk out of turn. ❏ ❏
   Rewrite: _____

2. Be considerate of others. ❏ ❏
   Rewrite: _____

3. Do not hit others. ❏ ❏
   Rewrite: _____

4. Respect the property of others. ❏ ❏
   Rewrite: _____

5. Do not use profanity. ❏ ❏
   Rewrite: _____

6. Listen quietly while others are speaking. ❏ ❏
   Rewrite: _____

7. Obey all school rules. ❏ ❏
   Rewrite: _____

Blackline 6.2

Setting the Climate

Classroom Rules and Consequences

Directions: Develop five rules and logical consequences for violating the rules that are appropriate for your students.

Teacher:_____ **Class/Grade:**_____ **Date:**_____

Rule #1: _____
Consequences   1.
               2.
               3.
               4.
               5.

Rule #2: _____
Consequences   1.
               2.
               3.
               4.
               5.

Rule #3: _____
Consequences   1.
               2.
               3.
               4.
               5.

Rule #4: _____
Consequences   1.
               2.
               3.
               4.
               5.

Rule #5: _____
Consequences   1.
               2.
               3.
               4.
               5.

Blackline 6.3

Behavior Checklist

Teacher:_____ **Class:**_____ **Date:**_____

Rules:	**Consequences:**
Rule #1 _____	1. _____
Rule #2 _____	2. _____
Rule #3 _____	3. _____
Rule #4 _____	4. _____
Rule #5 _____	5. _____

Write the dates of all violations in boxes under rule numbers.

Class Roll	Rule					Comments
	1	2	3	4	5	
1.						
2.						
3.						
4.						
5.						
6.						
7.						
8.						
9.						
10.						
11.						
12.						
13.						
14.						
15.						
16.						
17.						
18.						
19.						
20.						

Blackline 6.4

Setting the Climate

Brainstorming Web

Teacher:_____ Class:_____ Date:_____

Directions: Draw a web on the blackboard or on newsprint. Ask students to brainstorm a list of areas where rules are needed in order to ensure a cooperative climate.

Brainstorming Web

```
_____                          _____

_____                          _____
                    ┌─────────────┐
_____   │ Rules Needed │        _____
                    │ for Our Class│
_____   └─────────────┘         _____

_____                          _____
```

Beginning teachers may not realize that some of their actions or comments could be causing behavior problems. Mentors can help mentees become sensitive, proactive teachers who prevent many potential disturbances by establishing a comfortable classroom environment. If students feel valued and safe, they can focus on their learning.

Establishing a Cooperative, Responsible Classroom Environment

by **Kay Burke**

"I hate doing these geometry problems," groans Chuck. "Why do we need to know this for life? We spend half the class working on these theorems!"

"What's the problem, Chuck?" asks Mrs. Nordstrom.

"Math is boring," Chuck explodes.

"Now, Chuck," Mrs. Nordstrom replies. "Things are not boring—people who don't understand them just think they're boring."

"I understand the problems," shouts Chuck. "I just don't give a damn!"

"If you understand so much," says Mrs. Nordstrom through gritted teeth, her voice rising, "Why did you score a 54 percent on your last test?"

"Because I wanted to flunk—it was my personal best."

Mrs. Nordstrom angrily shouts, "All right, young man. You can just march yourself down to the principal's office right now."

"Great, I'd rather sit in the office all day than sit in this stupid room!"

Adapted from *What to Do with the Kid Who. . .* by K. Burke, pp. 89–95. © 2000 by SkyLight Training and Publishing.

Establishing a Cooperative, Responsible Classroom Environment

Creating the Climate

The climate of a classroom refers to the teacher-student and peer relationships. A positive climate is established when a teacher not only "engages students' imaginations but also convinces them that they are people of worth who can do something in a very difficult world" (Kohl as cited in Scherer 1998, p. 9).

Kohl (as cited in Scherer 1998) believes that the first big thing that makes a difference is respect. If teachers don't feel that their students have equal value to themselves, then they won't teach them much. Kohl also believes that humiliation is absolutely a sin. He feels that teachers need to deal with students who defy them, but humiliation has to go. Lyrics from the song "The Wall" by Pink Floyd represent this point: *We don't need no education / We don't need no thought control / No dark sarcasm in the classroom / Teacher leave the kids alone.* Kohl feels we do need some education, "but dark sarcasm has to be removed from the teacher's repertoire of strategies" (Kohl as cited in Scherer 1998, p. 9).

Publicly humiliating or embarrassing students does not help students learn from their mistakes. It could, however, make them try harder not to get caught and cause them to devise clever ways to get revenge on whomever embarrassed them.

Dealing with disruptive students in private, in a fair and consistent manner, and in a manner that maintains their dignity and self-esteem helps them develop an "internal locus of control" and responsibility. Students with an internal locus of control feel guilty when they misbehave, learn from their mistakes, are able to accept the consequences for their actions, and know they can control their actions in the future.

Dealing with disruptive students in front of their peers in an emotional outburst of frustration and anger lowers the students' self-concepts, decreases their desire to cooperate and succeed, and prevents them from developing their own sense of responsibility. They learn how to become defensive and use an "external locus of control" to blame others for their problems. Consequently, these students rarely accept responsibility for their own actions. Public reprimands, moreover, eventually

SkyLight Professional Development

destroy the positive climate in any classroom. Students do not feel free to engage in interactive discussion, contribute ideas, or share experiences if they are never sure when they will incur the teacher's wrath or become the object of the teacher's sarcasm or anger. Respecting the dignity of each and every student is essential for effective classroom management.

Teacher Behaviors

If students perceive that the teacher is treating them unjustly, they may label that teacher "unfair" or "the enemy." The seeds of insurrection may then be planted, causing a small behavior incident to escalate into a major discipline problem.

Teachers need to be careful in their enforcement of classroom rules and consequences. Sometimes the message can be fair, consistent, and positive, but the delivery system can be sarcastic, punitive, and negative.

The "Dirty Dozen" (see Figure 7.1) describes the types of teacher behaviors that can erode a positive classroom climate and undermine any discipline program—no matter how democratic. Teachers can send signals to individual students and to the whole class in both subtle and blatant ways that jeopardize the caring, cooperative classroom. It is remarkable how many people remember an incident from school in which they were treated unjustly. These incidents often become a "defining moment" in shaping their own character. Figure 7.2 can help educators analyze and process critical incidents that they remember from school; it is also presented at the end of this selection as a Blackline master.

Burke's "Dirty Dozen"

Teacher Behaviors That Can Erode the Classroom Climate

1. **Sarcasm**

   Students' feelings can be hurt by sarcastic put-downs thinly disguised as humor.

2. **Negative tone of voice**

   Students can "read between the lines" and sense a sarcastic, negative, or condescending tone of voice.

3. **Negative body language**

   A teacher's clenched fists, set jaw, quizzical look, or threatening stance can speak more loudly than any words.

4. **Inconsistency**

   Nothing escapes the students' attention. They are the first to realize the teacher is not enforcing the rules and consequences consistently.

5. **Favoritism**

   "Brown-nosing" is an art and any student in any class can point out the "teacher's pet" who gets special treatment.

6. **Put-downs**

   Sometimes teachers are not aware they are embarrassing a student with subtle put-downs or insults.

7. **Outbursts**

   Teachers are sometimes provoked by students and they "lose it." These teacher outbursts set a bad example for the students and could escalate into more serious problems.

8. **Public reprimands**

   No one wants to be corrected, humiliated, or lose face in front of his or her peers.

9. **Unfairness**

   Taking away promised privileges; scheduling a surprise test; "nitpicking" while grading homework or tests; or assigning punitive homework could be construed as "unfair."

10. **Apathy**

    Students do not want to be ignored. Teachers who forget students' names or appear indifferent will lose students' respect.

11. **Inflexibility**

    Teachers who never adjust homework assignments or test dates to meet the needs of their students appear rigid and uncaring.

12. **Lack of humor**

    Teachers who cannot laugh at themselves usually don't encourage students to take risks and make mistakes. Humorless classes lack energy.

Figure 7.1

Reflecting on the Dirty Dozen

Directions: Review the Dirty Dozen list of teacher behaviors and select one behavior that happened to you when you were a student. Write a short description of the incident.

Behavior: _____

Description: _____

_____

_____

_____

_____

_____

_____

Select one behavior that you may have used with your own students. Write a short description.

_____

_____

_____

_____

_____

_____

_____

_____

_____

Suggest another way either one of these incidents could have been handled. _____

_____

_____

_____

_____

_____

_____

_____

_____

Figure 7.2

Proactive Teachers

The effective classroom teacher engages in the "professional response" to a student's inappropriate question or comment by anticipating the types of problems that could occur in the classroom and developing a repertoire of strategies for solving these problems. This type of proactive approach to preventing discipline problems before they occur is far less time-consuming than the reactive approach where teachers expend all their energy trying to solve problems after they occur. Teachers can utilize the following procedures to engage in a proactive approach.

1. Anticipate Potential Behavior Problems

- Don't allow potential problem students to sit together or work together in groups.
- Arrange seating patterns so teacher can see and be close to all students.
- Give both verbal and written directions to eliminate confusion and frustration, which often lead to behavior problems.
- Structure assignments that are relevant, motivating, and developmentally appropriate.
- Allow enough time for students to complete assignments.
- Scan the class frequently to notice or respond to potential problems.
- Make allowances for students with learning disabilities or physical handicaps so they are not frustrated and overwhelmed.
- Encourage peer tutoring to help weaker students complete their work without becoming frustrated.
- Conference with students prone to behavior problems to find out if they have some personal or family problems that might be causing them to be upset or uncooperative.
- Talk with counselors or support personnel to find out about any previous behavior problems students might have experienced and get suggestions about how to best meet the individual needs of students.

SkyLight Professional Development

2. **Diffuse Minor Problems Before They Become Major Disturbances**

Proximity

- Move close to students when you sense a problem developing.

Student-Selected Time-Out

- Allow students to select a time-out from the class or the group. Let the agitated student go to a desk or chair in the corner of the room to collect his or her thoughts or calm down.

Teacher-Selected Time-Out

- Ask the student to go to the time-out area to complete work when his or her behavior is disrupting the group's activity.

3. **Address Disruptive Behaviors Immediately**

- Ask to speak with the student privately in the hall, after class, or after school.
- Ask the student to explain what he or she thinks the problem is.
- Send "I-messages" telling the student how his or her behavior affects you. For example, "I feel upset when I see you arguing with your group members."
- Try to identify the real problem.
- Remind students of the procedures or rules.
- Handle the problem quickly and calmly.
- Don't create a bigger disruption when attempting to solve problems.
- Don't "lose it" by overreacting and becoming angry.
- Remove the offender(s) from the class so the other students are not an audience.
- Provide students with choices, if possible. For example, "If you choose to work alone rather than with your group, you must complete the entire project by yourself."

The Last Resort: The Principal

Even if teachers provide quality lessons that stimulate students' ideas and relate to real-life situations, and even if they are proactive, there will always be that hard-core group of students who choose to disrupt the rest of the class because the class does not satisfy their needs or because their desire for attention, power, or recognition supersedes their need to learn.

It is the teacher's responsibility to make sure these disruptive students do not destroy the positive atmosphere of the class and cooperative spirit of the learning teams. If teachers do their best to anticipate potential behavior problems, diffuse minor problems before they become major disturbances, and address disruptive behaviors immediately, they should be able to counteract most problems. However, once the teacher has done everything possible to solve the problem and to control the student's negative behavior, he or she must resort to outside help—the administration. Sending the student to the principal is not a cop-out, unless, of course, it is done at the first sign of a problem.

Teachers should never relinquish their position of authority early on in a problem situation with a student or they will lose the respect of that student, and possibly the respect of the whole class. Once the teacher contacts the administrator, he or she is no longer in control; the administrator is. If, however, the teacher has exhausted his or her repertoire of strategies, the student's behavior has not improved, and the disruptive behavior is negatively influencing the entire class, the last resort becomes the next step. The student may also have to be referred to the school counselor, psychologist, special education coordinator, or social worker. It is important that teachers have accurate documentation of the student's behavior (dates, incidents, actions taken). It is also important for teachers to engage in a variety of problem-solving strategies to try to determine the real problem that might be causing the misbehavior.

GUIDEBOOK

Agree/Disagree Chart

Directions: Review the following statements about classroom climate and check if you "agree" or "disagree" with a statement.

Setting the Classroom Climate

	Agree	Disagree
1. The term *rules* sounds too dictatorial. It should be replaced with *Expectations* or *Principles*.		
2. Logical consequences are the same as punishments.		
3. Writing students' names on the board improves their behavior.		
4. A "time-out" area should be designated in a classroom.		
5. Sarcasm is effective in introducing humor to the classroom.		
6. Classroom management is basically behavior problem solving.		
7. Students should be sent to the principal for violating a rule.		
8. Teachers need to create the rules.		

Select one statement and provide the rationale for either agreeing or disagreeing with it.

Statement #:_____   **Rationale:** _____

_____

_____

_____

_____

_____

_____

Figure 7.3

Figure 7.3 is an agree/disagree chart where teachers can read the statement about setting the classroom climate and decide whether they agree or disagree. Establishing a comfortable classroom climate is the first step towards effective classroom management.

REFERENCES

Scherer, M. 1998. A conversation with Herb Kohl. *Educational Leadership* 56(1): 8-13.

Two Blackline masters are provided on the pages that follow:
- Reflecting on the Dirty Dozen
- Agree/Disagree Chart

The mentor can ask the protégé to complete both blacklines. The mentor can discuss the dirty dozen and the protégé's experience with the problem behaviors—encouraging the protégé to avoid the dirty dozen when teaching. The mentor can also help the protégé review his or her ideas about setting a good classroom climate and discuss the best way to create a positive climate for the protégé's students.

Reflecting on the Dirty Dozen

Directions: Review the Dirty Dozen list of teacher behaviors and select one behavior that happened to you when you were a student. Write a short description of the incident.

Behavior: _____

Description: _____

_____

_____

_____

_____

_____

_____

Select one behavior that you may have used with your own students. Write a short description.

_____

_____

_____

_____

_____

_____

_____

_____

_____

Suggest another way either one of these incidents could have been handled. _____

_____

_____

_____

_____

_____

_____

_____

_____

Blackline 7.1

Establishing a Cooperative, Responsible Classroom Environment

Agree/Disagree Chart

Directions: Review the following statements about classroom climate and check if you "agree" or "disagree" with a statement.

Setting the Classroom Climate

	Agree	Disagree
1. The term *rules* sounds too dictatorial. It should be replaced with *Expectations* or *Principles*.		
2. Logical consequences are the same as punishments.		
3. Writing students' names on the board improves their behavior.		
4. A "time-out" area should be designated in a classroom.		
5. Sarcasm is effective in introducing humor to the classroom.		
6. Classroom management is basically behavior problem solving.		
7. Students should be sent to the principal for violating a rule.		
8. Teachers need to create the rules.		

Select one statement and provide the rationale for either agreeing or disagreeing with it.

Statement #:_____ **Rationale:** _____

_____

_____

_____

_____

_____

Blackline 7.2

SkyLight Professional Development

Once behavior expectations have been established, teachers must also design lessons to teach the skills students need in order to meet those expectations. Mentors can guide new teachers in creating social skills lessons to help students engage in positive social interactions in whole-class and cooperative learning activities.

What Social Skills Do They Need?

by **James Bellanca and Robin Fogarty**

Lots of times you have to pretend to join a parade in which you are really not interested in order to get where you're going.
—Christopher Morley

In this selection, the goal is to create a cooperative classroom. To accomplish this goal, the teacher must develop each student's social skills. In short, she teaches them how to cooperate with each other to achieve their shared goal. Cooperative groups are the primary mechanism for students to improve their social skills.

Some students respond to the informal social skills woven into the classroom expectations, roles, and guidelines. Others require more formal direction in acquiring the cooperative social skills.

It is especially helpful to give more formal attention to social skill instruction with younger students and with students in "low tracks." These are the students who can profit most with direct instruction, guided practice, and constructive feedback.

Adapted from Chapter Three of *Blueprints for Achievement in the Cooperative Classroom,* 3rd ed., by J. Bellanca and R. Fogarty. © 2002 by SkyLight Training and Publishing.

What Social Skills Do They Need?

Deciding on Social Skills

How does a teacher decide which cooperative social skills to teach formally? Which ones are best done informally? The answers to these questions depend on the cooperative skill levels found in each classroom. Students who enter with strong interpersonal skills, either because they developed those at home or in a previous class, need less time on the basics and can advance to the more sophisticated skills.

Informal Instruction

For the informal instruction in social skills, the teacher will reinforce previously learned cooperative skills: roles (e.g., encourager, recorder); rules (e.g., 6" voices, one person talks); expectations (e.g., work on your attentive listening), processing (e.g., "Select a cooperative skill to practice and describe how you are improving"), and feedback (e.g., "I'm glad to see how quietly you moved into your teams"). Every activity, every lesson can be heightened by including informal, cooperative skill development within it.

Formal Instruction

For the formal instruction of cooperative skills, it is important that students

- understand the need and value of the skill,
- know the chief behavior indicators of the skill,
- know when to use the skill,
- practice the skill,
- reflect on improved use of the skill, and
- persist in refining the skill until it is automatic.

SkyLight Professional Development

A Focus on Forming Skills

What Skills Are Best Taught?

In the forming stage, individuals learn how to contribute to and benefit from teamwork. This stage includes learning

- how to move into a group,
- how to move out of a group,
- who talks in a group,
- who listens,
- how to help the group, and
- how to keep on task.

See Figure 8.1 for a chart to use to assess your class.

Assessing Your Class

THE FORMING SKILLS

Skill	Needed	Have	Comments
Move into a group			
Move out of a group			
One person talks at a time			
Stay with group			
Control volume of talk (3", 6", 12")			
Practice all roles			
Keep hands and feet to self			

Figure 8.1

What Social Skills Do They Need?

How to Move Into Groups

Let's consider how you might teach one of the basic forming skills—moving into groups. With a permanent seating arrangement for the groups there is little to worry about in moving desks. If however, desks are moved in and out of rows, then teach, practice, reinforce, and reflect on these model procedures:

1. Say, "Pick up your books and set them against the wall. Sit down." (Do one row at a time.)
2. Give each student a group assignment:
   - Who Is In Which Group? (Use cards with colored dots, group names, or another group assignment method.)
   - Who Has Which Role? (Assign roles appropriate for the lesson and the students: calculator, reader, encourager, etc.)

   Display the desired group pattern on the overhead or blackboard.
3. Say, "Move your seats so you are sitting with your new group."

   Invite the students to form their groups quietly. If the class is too noisy, stop the activity until all students are quiet; reinforce the class's quiet expectation and begin again.
4. Give positive reinforcement for a completed, quiet move and invite the students to gather their books or to get their work materials for today's task.
5. After the task is done, instruct students to put their materials back, to rearrange their desks (put diagram on overhead or blackboard), and to sit until they are dismissed.

Teaching Other Forming Skills

Determine which of the other forming skills on the list (Figure 8.1) will help your students work on task in a group. For instance, if you have a low tolerance for noise or a particular class is noisy, use a direct-instruction lesson to reinforce your expectations for quiet. Use your signal to get the class's attention. When all are quiet, give your expectation (speak in voices you can hear no more than six inches away); sit in a group and demonstrate a six-inch voice; guide practice until you can say "Great! You have it." When the class strays, repeat the cycles at the "teachable moment."

A Focus on Norming Skills

Every teacher deserves the norms of student-to-student interaction to be positive and encouraging. Unfortunately, the norms learned from TV's humor, sports figures, and the playground may be negative and discouraging. To change the norms from negative put-downs, disrespectful slurs, and inattention to good social skills, explicit attention from the teacher is needed.

One forming skill most practical to initiate in any classroom is encouraging. In the TV-saturated world of students, the art of the comic put-down makes peer encouragement a highly needed "basic" skill for the cooperative classroom.

Preparation

Solid formal instruction of a social skill requires the same careful preparation found in any procedural lesson (see Figure 8.2). To teach a social skill, first use a "hook." A hook, is usually a role play, a structured group experience, or a story that illustrates the social skill lesson (See the IALAC lesson at the end of this selection. Other hooks include people searches, agree/disagree statements, or think-pair-share). After the hook, create a T-chart that includes the words and behaviors common to the social skill (see Figure 8.3 for a sample). The T-chart, applicable to every cooperative social skill, helps students understand the specific behaviors that make up a chosen social skill. Instead of dealing with abstract words such as *encouragement* or *attentive listening,* the students work with specific behaviors. What does encouragement sound like? What does it look like?

What Social Skills Do They Need?

TEACHING SOCIAL SKILLS

Hook The hook lessons lay the groundwork. For the younger students and other students who lack the cooperative skills or thrive in a peer culture that reinforces negative social skills, more time and more energy on practice, reinforcement, and recognition of the essential cooperative skills are necessary. All students need some form of encouragement to develop these skills.

Teach Use a T-chart or web with the students. This will enable them, after the hook lesson, to generate the specific behaviors of the social skill. Do charts for both the acceptable behaviors (i.e., listening) and for the non-acceptable behavior (i.e., non-listening). Add behaviors the students miss from your preparation charts. Post the charts on the bulletin board or provide a copy for each student's notebook.

Practice Guided skill practice, massed in short bursts, is a necessary step after presenting the hook and teaching the basics. For instance, active listening pairs can practice with each other in three- to five-minute segments. Student A listens as student B shares an idea, explains a selected concept or describes an event. After the practice, A self-evaluates his/her listening practice. On the next day, they reverse roles. As the pairs develop their listening skills, begin to focus more and more on using course content as the subject for practice.

Extended practices give students a chance to reinforce the listening skill. Build a listening component into each lesson. In the criteria for lesson success, tell the students what is expected with the skill: For example, "I want to see at least five listening behaviors from each group" or "On your group evaluation, I expect you to report five examples of active listening."

Observe As students practice the desired social skills, the teacher or designated student observers watch for examples. To help with the observations, some teachers keep a checklist. While the groups work on task, the teacher records samples of the specified social skills. After the groups process their work, the teacher recognizes the positive examples he/she observed and encourages continued practice of the skills by all students.

Practice should continue until the social skill becomes automatic. This takes time. When the skill is first introduced with the hook, the students enter the first stage of change: awareness. If the hook catches them, they will perceive the need for the skill and increase commitment to improvement. After positive feedback they refine and refine until the skill becomes automatic.

Reflect Self-reflection helps students develop intrinsic motivation.

Figure 8.2

After creating the T-chart, you may choose to prepare a display. A large bulletin board celebrating encouragement with words and pictures, a model T-chart on the wall, or a T-chart handout provides a daily reminder.

As needed, practice the behaviors with a role play, simulation, or imbedded group task. Observe and record examples of students using the behaviors in practice. Conclude with a reflection using a stem (I like encouragement because . . .; encouragement is most helpful when . . .).

At some point in the putting together of cooperative groups, take time to give feedback on progress being made in becoming effective groups. This will help the class stay focused on setting the norm for positive interactions.

Obviously, students who already have the forming and norming skills well in hand do not need to spend time on these basics of cooperation. Share the expectations and unite the group teams with them—they will be ready to wade into the course content and to learn the more advanced social skills.

T-Chart

ENCOURAGEMENT

Sounds Like	Looks Like
Keep at it.	thumbs up
Atta girl, Atta boy!	pat on back
Way to go!	smile
Here's another way to look at it . . .	head nodding
Great idea.	beckoning hand
Keep trying.	
You're getting close.	

Figure 8.3

What Social Skills Do They Need?

A Focus on Advanced Social Skills

The forming and norming social skills are only the start. If students turn these skills into habits in a flash, as many do, they are ready to tackle the more advanced social skills. The more advanced the class becomes in its collaborations, the more opportunities appear for infusion of social skills into lesson designs. The more skilled students become with the social skills, the more productive and on-task the groups will function. The more "time on task" caused by skillful group work, the better the achievement results.

As explained earlier, social skills do not develop without deliberate, specific, and repeated attention. In teaching social skills, the explicit model outlined has proven most beneficial for the introduction of a skill. Integration of a skill and reflection on its use are the two keys most likely to open the door to groups best able to monitor their own behavior. In the chart entitled "Phases of Introduction of Social Skills," the six phases of the small-group process are outlined (see Figure 8.4). Coupled with each phase is a listing of suggested social skills appropriate for explicit attention during the instruction of that phase.

For example, it seems appropriate (and probably necessary) to teach students how to disagree with ideas, not people, as groups show evidence of storming. Similarly, as groups show signs of exquisite performance and become high-functioning teams, it is appropriate to target the more sophisticated skill of reaching consensus.

Although the charted skills are probably somewhat developmentally listed, individual situations dictate the depth and/or sequence of the actual teaching of social skills. Each teacher must decide on the final design of the social skill introductions. Reference to the chart is suggested only to help plan explicitly for the wide range of social skills needed.

As the social skill instruction develops throughout the year, explicit inclusion of skills from each of the categories is important. Thus, when trying to choose which social skills to teach, how many skills to include, and when to teach which skills, the categories may be helpful for picking the actual menu of items.

Phases of Introduction of Social Skills

PHASE	SOCIAL SKILLS Communication (C), Trust (T), Leadrship (L), Conflict Resolution (CR)	
Forming *to organize groups and establish behavior guidelines*	Use a 6" voice. (C) Listen to your neighbor. (C) Stay with the group. (C)	Heads together. (C) Do your job. (L) Help each other. (L)
Norming *to complete assigned tasks and build effective relationships*	Include all members. (L) Encourage others. (L) Listen with focus. (T)	Let all participate. (L) Respect each other's opinions. (T) Stay on task. (L)
Conforming *to promote critical thinking and maximize the learning of all*	Clarify. (C) Paraphrase ideas. (C) Give examples. (C)	Probe for differences. (CR) Generate alternatives. (CR) Seek consensus. (CR)
Storming *to function effectively and enable the work of the team*	Sense tone. (C) Disagree with idea not person. (CR) Keep an open mind. (T)	See all points of view. (CR) Try to agree. (CR Contribute own ideas. (L)
Performing *to foster higher-level thinking skills, creativity and depth intuition*	Elaborate on ideas. (C) Integrate ideas. (L) Justify ideas. (CR)	Extend ideas. (C) Synthesize. (L) Reach consensus. (CR)
Re-forming *to apply accross curriculum and transfer into life beyond the classroom*	Begin cycle of social skills again—each time: • New group is formed. • New member joins the group. • Member is absent from group. • New task is given. • Long absences occur.	

Figure 8.4

What Social Skills Do They Need?

The most successful teachers of cooperative learning are natural modelers of the cooperative social skills. These teachers go beyond modeling social skills in a "demo" lesson. They model positive social skills in all interactions with students. They speak softly, often with a "6-inch voice"; they establish eye-contact and focus their listening on what is said; they probe for differences in ideas, not the person. They avoid shouting at students, arguing, or dominating discussions. Most important, the students experience this high level of social skills in action and more easily copy what the teacher is doing. Thus, these teachers put in place the axiom, "Do as I do and as I say."

The caveat to all: Do not COVER social skills. Each skill is meant to be modeled, practiced, and used throughout the students' time in the classroom. One social skill mastered by the class each semester is more helpful than 20 "covered"! Less is more.

If teachers are under inordinant pressure to cover curriculum, it is sometimes difficult for them to see where social skills "fit." Let us say only this: whether a teacher takes the time to introduce the forming skills because those are needed for basic classroom management, or takes time to teach the more complex skills at the performing or norming stage, the pay off is always greater mastery of content. Sometimes it is necessary for a teacher to throw out miniscule facts in order to find the time. More likely, the improved social skills will enable more on-task, on-focus, concentrated student effort. The results of such effort and such increased student responsibility to learning are obvious not only for increased achievement, but also for an increase in the lifelong skills of collaborating with others.

Conclusion

Because cooperative learning teaches students by word and by example how to work well with others, it promotes higher student achievement. As a result of learning how to develop the social skills necessary for learning from the notion that "many hands together are better than one hand alone," students have increased support and assistance to meet the challenges of the curriculum, overcome obstacles to learning, and benefit from multiple points of view.

For the teacher, there are benefits beyond student achievement. When a teacher lays the foundation of a less stressful, more positive classroom culture, students help each other without bullying, violent interaction or annoying distractions. When the teacher builds the groups and works them through the stages of development, she expands the students' capabilities to work successfully in family and work collaborations throughout life.

Three sample lessons are provided on the pages that follow:
- Tell/Retell (elementary)
- IALAC (middle)
- The Nonlistening Challenge (secondary)

All three give ideas for teaching social skills. Protégés may adapt any of these lessons to their classrooms with guidance from their mentors. Mentors may also encourage protégés to create their own lessons for teaching specific social skills.

What Social Skills Do They Need?

BLUEPRINT: ELEMENTARY LESSON

Tell/Retell

SETTING UP THE SCAFFOLDING

To teach about attentive listening, prepare a bulletin board with an attentive listening theme. Show pictures of (a) a class attending to the teacher, (b) group members attending to each other, (c) a class attending to a visitor, and (d) a class attending to a student speaker.

Make and display a T-chart on the bulletin board.

ATTENTIVE LISTENING	
Sounds Like	**Looks Like**
1. "uh huh"	1. eyes alert and focused on talker
2. "I see."	2. mirroring emotions
3. clarifying questions	3. leaning forward or toward speaker
4. silence	4. head nods at right time
5. paraphrasing	5. taking notes
6.	6.
7.	7.
8.	8.

WORKING THE CREW

Gather students around and explain the bulletin board and chart. Have volunteers share how it feels to have someone's full attention. Solicit several answers. Demonstrate with the principal, another teacher, or a volunteer what attentive listening looks and sounds like.

Divide students into pairs. Instruct one student to share a fun adventure. Instruct the other to attend closely so he/she can repeat the story. Walk among the pairs and give a thumbs-up to each child seen listening.

Use this monitoring time to be aware of misbehaving students, especially during these times when interpersonal skills and social behavior are the focus. Be aware of "the kid who…" seeks attention, feels inadequate, makes the power play, is looking for revenge, or shows signs of emotional disturbances.

When a misbehaving student exhibits a deficit in a social skill, take time to address the social skill with clear, directed, and effective action. Say, for example, in this "Tell/Retell" lesson, one student is causing a lot of distraction during the partner interaction by clowning around and seeking the attention of the students around him/her. This is the teachable moment. You could begin with the strategy recognizing a student who is modeling the proper behavior. For example, standing near the attention seeker who is faking falling out of his chair to get attention from his partner and others, the teacher might say to a nearby pair: "I like the way you're positioned for good listening. Eye-to-eye, knee-to-knee is how attentive listening partners often sit."

By focusing on the desired modeled behavior and by telling explicitly what it looks like, the teacher cues the misbehaving student about two things: (1) modeling desired behavior gets the attention of the teacher, and (2) the desired behavior looks like this.

Although these actions seem like simple classroom management, by addressing the incident within the context of learning, the teacher adds power to the reinforcement strategy. Additionally, the teacher can talk about the incident or use the groups' reflection time to lead discussion on the idea of "seeking attention" as "clowning around."

REFLECTING ON THE DESIGN

To process affectively, conduct a brief sharing, then let several listeners tell the class what they heard in their partner interactions. Praise them for good listening. Have them tell how it felt to have someone listen so carefully.

To process the social skill of active listening, ask students to tell about someone they think is a good listener.

To process cognitively, continue to practice on succeeding days. Begin each practice with a review of the T-chart. End it with praise to the attentive listeners.

After several short practices, have a discussion in which the class talks about (a) why listening attentively is a good idea and (b) what times in class and at home are important for attentive listening. This metacognitive talk helps students transfer the social skill beyond the lesson.

What Social Skills Do They Need?

BLUEPRINT: MIDDLE SCHOOL LESSON

IALAC

SETTING UP THE SCAFFOLDING

Use Sidney Simon's IALAC (I Am Lovable And Capable) strategy or tell the students a unique version of the IALAC story using the following sample. Hold the IALAC sign.

(Name) , age _____ , woke up one school morning looking at _____ pajama top. _____ saw a giant, neon sign. It flashed on and off, IALAC. _____ knew at once this meant "I Am Lovable And Capable." _____ dressed and ran quickly to the kitchen. _____ was very excited. Before _____ could speak, _____ sister said, "You pea-brain, (rip off a corner of the sign) what did you do with my new jacket?" "Nothing," _____ said. "Man," whined _____ sister, "_____ is a jerk." (rip) "_____," said _____ unhappy mother. "You oughta know better. Why can't you use your brain (rip) once in a while. Your big brother would never do nothing so stupid." (rip) "But Mom," _____ said, "I . . . ." "Don't sass me back," said _____ mother. "You are such a smart mouth." (rip) _____ saw _____ sister smurk-ing. "Smart mouth, smart mouth." (rip, double rip)

By the time _____ left for the school bus, one-half of IALAC was ripped. On the school bus, George Burns said _____ was an idiot (rip), cry baby, and jerk (rip). _____ sister laughed each time. (triple rip)

In the first class period, Mrs. Smartzolla asked to put _____ homework problem on the board. _____ forgot a (name item) in the formula. "_____," she moaned, "how slow can you be? I've told you a thousand times." (rip)

In language arts, Mr. Thomas barked at _____ for getting the lowest score on the vocabulary quiz. (rip) He read how _____ had misspelled _____ to the whole class and said sarcastically, "I guess no one could ever accuse you of a gorgative brain." (rip) Everyone laughed. (rip)

By the end of the day, _____ went home with a very small IALAC sign. _____ was very upset.

SkyLight Professional Development

*The next day, _____ woke to find IALAC on _____ pajamas, but
very small. _____ hoped that today would be better. _____ wanted
to keep _____ IALAC so much.*
(Continue this story with additional IALAC demolition.)

WORKING THE CREW

After the story, place students into groups of five, each group with one
piece of 3" x 5" newsprint and a marker. Appoint a recorder in each
group to write down all the different ways they have their IALACs ripped.
After five minutes, ask several recorders to share samples.

Instruct the groups to make a second list: What things can they do or
say to increase people's IALACs? After five minutes, ask for samples.

Ask each group to pick the three best IALAC builders from its list.
Make an unduplicated class list to hang in the classroom.

REFLECTING ON THE DESIGN

To process affectively, have students finish the following statement:

It feels good when . . . .

To process socially, ask students to take time today to use positive
statements with a family member.

To process cognitively, post the encouragement T-chart (Figure 8.3)
and discuss how the class can use it to build each other's IALACs. On succeeding days, use the following ideas for practice.

To process metacognitively, ask students to discuss:

- what they did well in the groups, and
- what they would do differently next time to help their groups

BLUEPRINT: SECONDARY SCHOOL LESSON

The Nonlistening Challenge

SETTING UP THE SCAFFOLDING

Divide the class into pairs. Ask students to think of a recent time when someone important paid close attention to them. As they tell you how they knew they were getting attentive listening, make a T-chart for attentive listening.

ATTENTIVE LISTENING	
Sounds Like	**Looks Like**
1. "uh huh"	1. eyes alert and focused on talker
2. "I see."	2. mirroring emotions
3. clarifying questions	3. leaning forward/toward speaker
4. silence	4. head nods at right time
5. paraphrasing	5. taking notes

Identify the oldest student in each pair. Those students are As. The younger student in each pair is B. Invite A to listen to the first instructions. Each A is to think of a time in the past year when someone did not listen. What happened? How did it feel? The As are to prepare their stories while the Bs are given instructions.

WORKING THE CREW

Invite the Bs to review the T-chart. Now say, "Now that you have reviewed how to behave when you listen with attention, you are to do your 100 percent, absolute, total best NOT to listen to your partner's story! You are to model non-listening behaviors." Require these guidelines: (1) all must stay in the room, (2) speakers do your best to tell the story, (3) don't hurt each other, and (4) stop when the teacher gives the signal (e.g., lights off, hands up).

Move around the room and note the students' behavior. Be aware of genuine misbehavior in students, especially during these times in which interpersonal skills and social behavior are the focus. Be aware of "the kid who..." seeks attention, feels inadequate, makes the power play, is looking for revenge, or shows signs of emotional disturbances. When a misbehaving student exhibits a deficit in a social skill, take time to address the social skill with clear, directed, and effective action.

Even better, in the "Non-listening" lesson activity you have asked students to deliberately demonstrate poor listening skills. Now, take advantage of this activity. Find the student who takes over the partner interview as the dialogue becomes very one-sided. This is the teachable moment to address the question, "What do you do with the kid who...takes over?"

Moving this student into a leadership role seems to be an applicable strategy for this situation. For example, in the midst of this partner interaction, tell the class to "freeze frame." Suggest that to reinforce the roles of each partner, one pair will model or role play an interaction. Select the pair with the partner who has "taken over" and have them model the desired actions. Surprisingly, the misbehavior disappears instantly and the desired behavior is modeled in true leadership style. However, since the non-listening activity is intentionally set up to focus on misbehavior, this "power play" might be tried by others.

By designating a leadership role for the "offender" in front of the class, the "power play" in the small group is no longer as interesting to the misbehaving student. So be sure to highlight the reason the strategy of giving a leadership role works. In addition, this same student has actually modeled the very behavior he/she was lacking. Although this may be simple classroom management, by addressing this incident within the context of social skill instruction, the teacher adds power to the situation with positive reinforcement. She/he also can talk about the incident or use the groups' reflection time to lead discussion on the idea of power plays as taking over the group.

After two minutes, stop the activity. Have each pair shake hands, with the Bs apologizing to the As.

For affective processing, conclude with a discussion of the positive effects on a speaker and a listener when attention goes both ways.

What Social Skills Do They Need?

REFLECTING ON THE DESIGN

To process the social skill of listening, have students describe a TV character who is a good listener.

To process cognitively, put a double T-chart for non-listening on the board. What did non-listening look like, sound like, and feel like?

For metacognitve processing, discuss with the class instances when they may have experienced the same negative feelings caused by non-listening.

SkyLight Professional Development

Mentors can help new teachers recognize the cause of many behavior problems and develop a repertoire of problem-solving strategies. Since classroom management problems cause so many teachers to leave the profession, it is critical that protégés recognize potential discipline problems and address them appropriately.

Students with Behavior Problems

by **Kay Burke**

Addressing Behavior Problems

When students display inappropriate behavior, they do so because they have the mistaken goal that it will get them the recognition and acceptance they want (Dreikers et al. as cited in Vaughn, Bos, and Schumm 2000, p. 81).

Behavior problems constitute student behaviors that cause disruptions in the class. This type of behavior can be directed at other students or the teacher, and can include student behaviors such as talking when another student or the teacher is talking, name calling, fighting, arguing, throwing things, or getting up out of one's seat. Although any of these behaviors is enough to disrupt a classroom, they can be controlled by a proactive teacher.

Curwin and Mendler (1988) proposed the 80-15-5 model where they estimated that 80 percent of students in most classes never or rarely break the classroom rules and cause disruptions. They estimated that about 15 percent of students break rules on a regular basis and 5 percent are chronic rule breakers. However, Walsh (as cited in Levin and Nolan 1996) reports that some teachers spend as much as

Students with Behavior Problems

30 to 80 percent of their time addressing discipline problems. It is evident that the successful teacher of the twenty-first century needs to be able to manage students in order to maximize the time spent on learning. With the increased emphasis on high-stakes standardized tests, standards, and accountability, teachers must increase time-on-task to prepare students to meet rigorous academic goals.

Ripple Effect

Teachers are concerned not only with addressing student disruptions, but also with the "ripple effect" (Kounin as cited in Levin and Nolan 1996). The ripple effect results from the initial misbehavior, the methods the teacher uses to curb the misbehavior, and the resultant behavior of the targeted student. "Studies have shown that rough and threatening teacher behavior causes student anxieties, which lead to additional disruptive behaviors from on-looking students. However, students who see that disruptive students comply with the teacher's control technique rate their teacher as fairer and are themselves less distracted from their classwork than when they observe unruly students defying the teacher" (Smith as cited in Levin and Nolan 1996). There are, therefore, many complex dynamics that come into play when a teacher addresses even a minor behavior disruption.

At-Risk Students

Educators often use the term *at risk* to describe a particular category of students. Slavin (as cited in Manning and Baruth 1995), referring only to academically at-risk learners, defines *at risk* as referring to students who, on the basis of several risk factors, are unlikely to graduate from high school. Yet, educators are also confronted with children and adolescents who have other at-risk factors due to "health problems, substance use, disabilities, socioeconomic status (SES), attempted suicides, and other behaviors such as experimenting with drugs and sexual activity" (Manning and Baruth 1995, p. 6).

The difficult challenge is labeling students because at-risk conditions are not clear cut and what causes one student to be at risk may not affect other students the same way. Short, Short, and Blanton (1994) discuss how students who are low achievers in school activities are described as at-risk students. Some of the characteristics they describe for an at-risk child include students who have not mastered basic skills, have been retained, are below grade level on test scores, have a poor attendance record, have a record of suspensions, qualify for free or reduced lunch, or have a history of high mobility. In addition, at-risk students could have experienced child abuse or neglect; abused substances; have experienced racial, cultural, or gender bias; or come from a dysfunctional family. "A large proportion of school-age children either are or will be poor, multicultural/minority, and from nontraditional homes— all characteristics that have been related to school and social failure" (Short, Short, and Blanton 1994, p. 75).

Even though the characteristics of at-risk students are mostly extrinsic to the child, they still have a profound effect on the development and performance of the student in school. Moreover, at-risk students often display characteristics that distinguish them from the rest of their peer group. This difference can cause tremendous social pressures that result in their not fitting in with the social structure of the class and exhibiting recurrent discipline problems in school (Short, Short, and Blanton 1994).

Teachers have to be aware of the "baggage" many students bring to school each day. They need to be as fair and consistent as possible with maintaining high expectations for all students and enforcing classroom procedures, rules, and consequences. They must also, however, be aware of students' situations and the philosophical idea that "fair is not always equal," and each student should be handled with some consideration, respect, and flexibility, if possible.

Identifying Antecedents

The events or conditions that immediately precede instances of problem behavior are called antecedents (Kauffman, Hallahan, Mostert, Trent, and Nuttycombe 1993). Teachers can keep an anecdotal record or written notes to describe a pattern of

Students with Behavior Problems

when, where, and under what conditions the behavior most often occurs.

For example, if Jimmy usually becomes rude and obnoxious right before a major test, the teacher might have a private conference with him to find out why. Maybe he can't read the directions or he feels inadequate. Maybe he can't handle the time constraints of a test and would like more time. Maybe he can't understand the multiple-choice format and would do better on a performance task that demonstrates what he actually knows rather than how well he guesses.

Effective teachers look for patterns to identify specific events, times of the day, or activities that cause students to act out. One event that often causes disruptions is assigning students to groups. If Kathy hates Jenny because of a problem with an old boyfriend, she may cause a disruption to avoid working with Jenny in a cooperative project. Obviously, teachers cannot anticipate every potential problem, but the proactive teacher can diffuse potential problems before they become major problems.

Coercive Interaction

Kauffman, Hallahan, Mostert, Trent, and Nuttycombe (1993) discuss the typical situations that occur when a pupil finds a teacher's expectations and demands aversive or unpleasant. The teacher, in turn, finds the student's refusal to follow his or her order also aversive and therefore restates the demand and adds a threat or punishment as an "incentive." The student then feels challenged in front of his or her peer group and becomes even louder, more obnoxious, and more threatened, causing the teacher to respond with more severe threats of punishment. This type of coercive interaction continues until the teacher "wins" and the student backs down, which sometimes is temporary and then the student continues to seek revenge on the teacher for "beating" him or her in public. Another typical situation results in the teacher backing down and not following through with the threat, in which case the student wins. In this case, sometimes the teacher is "out to get the student" the rest of the year because he or she lost face in

GUIDEBOOK

Coercive Interaction

Teacher asks student to complete page of math problems.
Student says, "I don't know how to do this crap!"
Teacher says, "Yes you do, we just did some problems like these yesterday. Get started now."
Student slams book closed, saying "Ain't doin' it!"
Teacher goes to student's desk, opens book, hands student pencil, says in angry tone, "Get started now!"
Student shoves book off desk.
Teacher squeezes student's shoulder, growls, "Pick that book up, young man!"
Student jumps to feet, says, "Get your hands off me, bitch! You pick it up! You can't make me do nothin'!"
Teacher yells, "That's it! I've had enough of this! Pick that book up and get to work now or you're outta here to the office!"

Kauffman, Hallahan, Mostert, Trent, and Nuttycombe 1993, p. 31. Reprinted with permission.

Figure 9.1

front of the class. The best situation that can occur is a win-win situation where both parties compromise, save face, and address the real cause of the problem and possible solutions in private. Figure 8.1 represents a typical coercive classroom interaction. Skillful teachers can avoid coercive interactions and recognize when students are baiting them to seek attention or engage in a power struggle.

Students Who Seek Attention

Glenn gets up from his desk and slowly walks down the aisle to the pencil sharpener and starts sharpening a long pencil. Each time he finishes sharpening, he puts the pencil inside again until it becomes a stub.

"Sit down," yells Mrs. Martinez. "We're trying to work here and you're not supposed to be out of your desk."

"I'm just trying to sharpen my pencil," Glenn announces loudly to the entire class. "Is that a crime? Excuse me for living!"

Students with Behavior Problems

Mrs. Martinez walks over to Glenn and whispers quietly, "Glenn, the class is working on their group art project and your group really needs your help."

Glenn reluctantly rejoins his group and proceeds to draw a happy face on the back of Mary's black sweater with a piece of hot-pink colored chalk.

"You jerk," shrieks Mary. "When are you going to grow up?"

Glenn laughs and looks around the room to see all the students and Mrs. Martinez staring at him.

Mrs. Martinez walks over and taps Glenn on the shoulder and they both walk into the hall.

Solving the Problem

Many misbehaving students are seeking extra attention. Albert (1989) says that all people need a certain amount of attention to feel like they belong and are an important part of the social group. "In contrast, students who misbehave for attention are never satisfied with a normal amount. They want more and more, as if they carry around with them a bucket labeled 'attention' that they expect the teacher to fill" (p. 26).

Attention seekers are students who seek independence, but spend a great deal of their time complaining to others that they cannot control what is happening in their lives. "They see themselves as victims of circumstance and strive to gain attention by keeping adults busy with them" (Dinkmeyer, McKay, and Dinkmeyer 1980, p. 252).

Many attention seekers are discouraged students who may become obnoxiously loud and silly or may resort to immature acts like pushing books off a desk or trying to trip someone to get noticed. Attention seekers are like stage performers; they require an audience. They do get noticed, but many of them eventually get rejected by their peers and their teacher, who grow tired of their attempts to always be in the limelight. The attention seeker's idea of success is to be on stage, even if their actions violate the dignity and rights of other students and earn him or her the hostility of those who feel attacked or violated (Dinkmeyer and Losoncy 1980). In the elementary grades, attention seekers usually gear their performance towards the teacher, but as they move to upper grades, they prefer a wider audience that includes their classmates, guidance counselors, administrators, and sometimes the entire school community (Albert 1989).

Appropriate Attention

The origins of attention-seeking behavior can range from students not receiving enough attention at home to students not knowing how to ask for attention in an appropriate manner. The greatest challenge for teachers is to change the behavior of the attention seeker by giving him or her as little attention as possible when the misbehavior occurs. Bellanca and Fogarty (1991, p. 73) recommend the following strategies to teachers:

- Highlight students who are behaving appropriately.
- Move the student out of the spotlight by giving him an errand to run.
- Distract the student with a question.
- Attend to the attention seeker positively when he is on task.

By encouraging attention seekers to succeed in individual or group work and by noticing and encouraging their accomplishments, teachers and students can reinforce appropriate behavior with positive attention. The goal is to encourage attention seekers to strive for positive attention from peers and teachers rather than resort to negative attention to fulfill their needs.

Since one method to prevent students from seeking attention is to identify the goal of the misbehavior, teachers should help students to analyze their own behavior. The Newspaper Model (see Figure 9.2) allows attention seekers to analyze their actions and reflect on the causes and effects of their behavior. A Blackline master of a Newspaper Model form teachers can use with their students is provided at the end of this selection (Blackline 9.1). Teachers should work with students to fill out the form in order to discuss and reflect on the process.

MENTORING

The Newspaper Model

Ask the student to state what he or she thinks the problems is, and describe his or her take on who is involved, what usually happens, when the problem occurs, where it occurs, and why it happens. The attention seeker should write a paragraph about the situation and share the paragraph with others involved in the problem, taking steps to stop the problem.

Name: _Glenn_ Date: _Feb. 3_

Problem: _I got in trouble for sharpening my pencil and drawing on Mary's sweater._

Who	What	When	Where	Why
(me) Glenn	Caused a disturbance by sharpening my pencil and drawing on Mary's sweater.	Tuesday Feb. 3 during 5th period	In Mrs. Martinez's art class at Oak School	Because I was mad that the teacher and Mary yelled at me.

Write a paragraph describing your view of what happened.

I got mad because John and Mary think they are better than me. They never use my ideas when we meet in groups. They are always calling me names and putting me down. I went to sharpen my pencil to get away from the group. Then I got mad when Mary laughed when I got in trouble. I showed the class who got the last laugh.

Signed: _Glenn_

Have another group member write a paragraph about the situation.

I called Glenn a jerk because he is always fooling around instead of helping. I know I shouldn't call him names, but I get real frustrated with him. I laughed at him when Mrs. Martinez yelled at him because I told him not to do it. I get very angry at him.

Signed: _Mary_

Figure 9.2

SkyLight Professional Development

Educators must remember that the number of students seeking attention will probably increase commensurate with the lack of attention students may be experiencing in their families and the large sizes of classes and schools. When students have to compete for attention each day, they may resort to more violent ways to capture the attention of their parents, teachers, classmates, and the media.

Other Strategies Teachers Can Use with Students Who Seek Attention

- Help the student find an area where she can shine. Find a specific interest or strength she has so that she can get attention in a positive way.
- Find the student a study buddy. Sometimes a student who lacks friends tries to compensate by acting out.
- Give the student an option of a short time-out period. He can go to a corner of the room and cool down or write in a journal about his feelings.
- Analyze the newspaper model to see when, where, and why most incidents occur. Remember to review the antecedents or context. If incidents usually arise from the student being involved with certain people or situations, try to avoid placing the student in those situations.
- When a student does something well, encourage her.
- When a student raises his hand, call on him quickly to give him positive attention for an answer or for trying to answer a question.
- Give the student legitimate positive attention by allowing her to run errands, lead the pledge, clean the board, collect papers, or take part in other positions of responsibility and honor. Be careful to rotate these privileges so the other students don't resent her.
- Have a secret signal to give the student from across the room to remind him when he is doing something to get attention.

Students with Behavior Problems

Students Who Seek Power

Mrs. Bradley returns the students' English tests and then asks if there are any questions.

"This sucks!" exclaims Brian. "You can't take off points for misspellings. We weren't allowed to use dictionaries!"

"You should know how to spell the words you write. I take off five points for every error."

"You can't do that!" Brian yells, moving forward in his desk. "This test was on short stories and we were supposed to describe the plots. Who cares if we misspelled a few words. You missed the point of the test! We didn't get to use spell check!"

"Excuse me, young man," Mrs. Bradley shrieks as her face turns red. "This is my class and I will be the one who decides what I will and will not grade!"

"This sucks," mutters Brian. "I want to go to my counselor to get transferred to Mrs. Brown's English class."

"You're not getting a pass from me," counters Mrs. Bradley.

"I don't need a pass—I'm outta here." Brian grabs his backpack and kicks his desk before he bolts from the room.

The other students glare at Mrs. Bradley in silence.

Solving the Problem

> I believe that the need for power is the core—the absolute core—of almost all school problems (Glasser as cited in Gough 1987, p. 658).

Students who seek independence sometimes engage in power conflicts with adults because they are determined not to do what adults want. Curwin and Mendler (1988) warn teachers not to get caught in a power trap: "Commit yourself to avoiding power struggles, even if it means initially backing down. Remember that continuation of a power struggle makes you look foolish and out of control. You must be prepared to see long-term victory (a cooperative, positive classroom climate) as more important than short-term winning" (p. 105).

Glasser (1986) feels that students, even good students, don't feel important in school because no one listens to them.

Moreover, students who receive poor grades and are considered discipline problems cannot feel important from the standpoint of academic performance and acceptance. Glasser asserts that students would work harder in school if they had more freedom and fun. Mendler (1997) says "it is estimated that 70 to 80 percent of challenging student behavior in school is primarily attributable to outside factors such as dysfunctional families, violence in our culture, the effects of drugs and alcohol, and fragmented communities" (p. 4). Yet, teachers cannot abrogate their responsibility for controlling student behavior in their classrooms by blaming it on outside forces. The challenge is to teach all students.

Most often, the power base in schools is tilted in favor of the teachers. Teachers have the power to threaten students and are able to back up those threats with minus points, minutes in the time-out area, detention, notes to parents, suspensions, expulsion, and the ultimate weapon—failure. Despite all the power teachers have, Glasser (1986) says that half the students still won't work because they don't feel they have any control over their lives. They are discouraged because they have so little to say about what they learn, when they learn it, and how they learn it. Students are discouraged and they don't have the patience to wait it out until teachers and the school system give them more say in their education. Power seekers vent this frustration through the use of temper tantrums, verbal tantrums, and quiet noncompliance (Albert 1989).

More and more schools are recognizing the need to empower students by allowing them to be involved in setting classroom rules and having some choice in what they study and how they will be assessed. "Students also need to learn to look for more effective behaviors while they wait, but they have less power over their lives than adults and little confidence that the school will change for the better. If we can restructure schools so that they are more satisfying, we can expect many more students to be patient when they are frustrated" (Glasser 1986, p. 55). The following tactics (see Figure 9.3) can be used by teachers to avoid getting pulled into a power struggle.

Tactics Teachers Can Use with Power Seekers

- Don't grab the hook. Teachers should not fall into the power trap, especially in front of the class.
- Avoid and defuse direct confrontations.
- Listen to the problem in private.
- Recognize the student's feelings.
- Privately acknowledge the power struggle.
- Do not embarrass students publicly.
- Give the students choices in their academic work.
- Place the power seeker in a leadership role.
- Encourage independent thinking, but not anarchy!

Figure 9.3

Students who seek power often try to dominate the entire class and their groups. If they cannot control the class, the teacher, or the school, they might consider their cooperative group as their personal power base. Teachers should monitor the roles assigned to group members and make sure power seekers are fulfilling their assignments without trying to take control of the entire group.

Another strategy teachers can use is to review the specific roles assigned to each group member and the responsibilities of each of these roles. Teachers can also remind students that group roles are rotated so everyone can get a chance to be the organizer or the group leader. If the tasks are structured so that they allow a great deal of choice, creativity, and freedom, power seekers should be satisfied that they do, in fact, have some control over their lives. This can help them to learn how to develop positive leadership qualities rather than negative dictatorial traits.

Figure 9.4 shows the phases in a power struggle.

SkyLight Professional Development

Phases of a Power Struggle

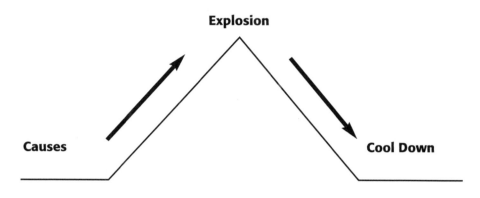

Figure 9.4

Figure 9.5 shows how the student and the teacher in this scenario analyze what they could have done differently to prevent a power struggle. A Blackline master of a form teachers can use with their own students is provided at the end of this selection (see Blackline 9.2). This graphic organizer (developed by B. Wiedmann of SkyLight Professional Development), can help teachers and students analyze the "hot points" or "key words and actions" that can cause a minor comment or incident to escalate into a full-scale power struggle from which neither the teacher nor the student can emerge victorious.

Power-seeking students constantly challenge teachers by trying to prove they are in control of issues such as tardiness, incomplete work, making noises, gum chewing, or muttering under their breath. Albert (1989) reminds teachers, "Often power-seeking students don't act out until they're assured of an audience. We [teachers] fear that if we lose a public battle, we'll be labeled a 'loser' by the entire class until school is out in June. The pressure of having to handle such a difficult situation with so much at stake in front of an audience adds greatly to our discomfort."

MENTORING

Phases of a Power Struggle

The teacher and the student involved in an altercation should fill out the form to find out what they did to provoke the struggle and what they can do in the future to prevent or resolve the problem.

Explosion

Causes

1. Mrs. Bradley deducted points for spelling errors.

2. Brian swore at her.

3. Mrs. Bradley yelled at Brian.

Brian defies Mrs. Bradley and storms out of the class.

Cool Down

1. Mrs. Bradley calms down and returns to the next lesson.

2. Brian meet with his counselor.

3. The counselor schedules a meeting with both of them.

What the teacher could have done to prevent the problem:
I should have told the students my criteria for grading before the test. I should have taken Brian out in the hall when he blew up.

What the student could have done to prevent the problem:
I should have asked to speak to Mrs. Bradley after class in private. I should not have lost my temper in class.

Resolution to problem:
Both Mrs. Bradley and Brian will talk to the class. Mrs. Bradley will promise to share her grading procedures prior to the test. Brian will apologize for his language and behavior. He will serve two detentions for violating school policy. Both will make an effort to conduct all disagreements in private—not in front of the class.

Teacher: Mrs. Bradley   Student: Brian   Date: Oct. 4

Other Strategies Teachers Can Use with Students Who Seek Power

- Keep cool and remain calm. The power-seeking student often tries to excite and anger the teacher and fellow students.

- Isolate the student from other group members or classmates. Don't allow a confrontation to erupt where people say and do things they later regret.

- Allow the student some time to cool down and get herself together. Let her go to a private area (office, media center, counselor, time out) so she can compose herself.

- Defuse his anger by saying, "I see your point" or "I know how you must feel," but then state what you think is necessary.

- Delay the issue by saying, "You can stay in your seat now and I'll consider giving you a pass later."

- Conference with the student to find out if any personal or family problems are making her anxious or belligerent. Sometimes the blow-up is not caused by the minor incident that precipitated it; it is because of personal problems.

- Write a contract with the student to brainstorm alternative ideas he might try when he is upset and wants to take control of the class or the group.

- Try to give him a leadership position in one of the next class activities. He can then exercise his leadership role in a positive way, rather than a negative way.

- Reinforce anything the student does that is positive. Encourage her actions when she maintains her cool.

- Have the student keep a Power Problem Journal to record what specific things upset him. The student will get time to process his feelings and reflect on his behavior. Self-analysis is a powerful tool in redirecting behavior.

Students with Behavior Problems

Students Who Seek Revenge

Coach Carden passes out the history test papers and proceeds to lecture the class.

"You must not care about passing this class and getting into college. These tests are pathetic! Did anyone here bother reading the chapter on the Civil War?" he asks sarcastically.

Rick stares at his 62 percent score and doesn't say a word. Then he suddenly crumbles his paper into a ball and tosses it towards the garbage can. It misses!

"Some basketball player you are," scoffs Coach Carden. "I'm glad I'm not your coach."

"I might not be a basketball player after I get my grade for this class. This sucks!" yells Rick.

"What did you say? You know I don't tolerate that kind of language in this class. See me after school today for an hour detention. We'll practice polite conversation."

"You can go to hell!" Rick shouts. "I have practice after school. You can't make me stay."

"Oh yeah, we'll see about that. You'll stay or you'll be suspended and miss a few games!" replies Coach Carden.

"That's not fair. You can't flunk the whole class and you can't make me stay in this sorry excuse for a class. I'm out of here."

Rick storms out of the room shouting, "We'll see what my parents and my coach say when they hear about this. My dad's a lawyer! We'll see you in court!"

Solving the Problem

Sometimes power seekers who never satisfy their need for power become revenge seekers to get back at the person or persons who thwarted their quest for power. Usually the revengeful student is trying to retaliate for something hurtful said by a parent, teacher, or peer, or for some injustice or unfair deed. Albert (1989) says these students often sulk or scowl even when not lashing out. They put teachers on edge because teachers are never sure when these students will retaliate.

The most important thing teachers can do for students who are seeking revenge is to help them rebuild positive relationships with the teacher or the class. It may be difficult for teachers to build a caring relationship with someone who has announced to the whole class that they "suck," but it is important. The social skill of encouragement needs to be emphasized, and teachers should monitor group activities to make sure the revenge seeker is included. The student who seeks revenge should be taught how to express his or her hurt or anger appropriately by talking to the teacher or his or her peers to resolve the problem. Teachers themselves can use the following tactics (see Figure 9.6) with revenge seekers to encourage positive behavior and to reduce power struggles.

Tactics Teachers Can Use with Revenge Seekers

- Avoid sarcasm or put-downs.
- Do not confront the student in front of her peers.
- Don't seek revenge on revenge seekers.
- Listen carefully to his problems (probe for causes).
- Form a positive relationship with the student.
- Encourage the student when she behaves appropriately.
- Ask the student to keep a journal to process feelings and analyze the causes for his anger.
- Admit mistakes.
- Use frequent teacher-student conferences to monitor behavior.

Figure 9.6

Revenge seekers need to be defused or else their hidden agenda may torpedo the class. When this happens, the other students can become resentful and distrustful of the revenge seeker. As a result, the revenge seeker compounds his or her personal problems by alienating peers as well as the teacher.

The revenge seeker's hidden agenda can snowball into a personality problem that can serve to brand the student as a "bully," "incorrigible," or a "loner" for the rest of the year or the rest of his or her schooling. Teachers need to take time from the textbook and curriculum to allow students to process their emotions. Teachers can do this by conferencing with the student, calling in a counselor or another teacher to talk to the student, having the student keep a diary or journal to record events that trigger an outburst, and analyzing different responses.

If students are not happy, satisfied, and accepted in the classroom, they will continue to disrupt learning and interfere with group interactions until their personal needs are met—sometimes at a very extreme level. For example, the violence across American schools, especially in Columbine, Colorado, in 1999, can be linked to students who were enraged. When enraged students kill, they are trying to extort revenge on the person or persons who enraged or embarrassed them or treated them disrespectfully, or anyone else who happens to be in their path. There is a strong link between student revenge seekers and school violence.

Teachers can use a Divided Journal (see Figure 9.7) to allow both themselves and students to reflect on what they may have said or done in anger and propose another way they could approach the problem if it occurs again. Sometimes these journals help teachers learn more about the inappropriateness of their actions and how their actions could have escalated a minor incident into a showdown in which both parties try to save face with the rest of the class. The ultimate revenge a teacher can retaliate with is failure, but students should not suffer academically for their poor behavior. The problem needs to be addressed so it doesn't distract from learning.

A Blackline master at the end of this selection offers a blank Divided Journal form teachers can use with their students (see Blackline 9.3). Reflection, which is the focus of the Journal, is a powerful tool to help adults, teenagers, and even young children process their feelings and analyze their actions in private.

Other Strategies Teachers Can Use with Students Who Seek Revenge

- Use I-messages: "When I see you losing your temper, I feel upset because . . ."
- Ask for a conference with the student and ask to have a counselor present as an objective observer.

Divided Journal

The teacher and the student need to process what happened by describing the incident and reflecting on what they would do differently. They should discuss their reactions and try to arrive at a mutually beneficial compromise.

Student: _Rick_ Date: _April 5_	Upon Reflection Date: _April 6_
Description of What Happened	**What I Would Do Differently**
I was angry because I studied hard for the test and Coach was yelling about how we weren't going to get into college. *I freaked out and threw my test away. It upset him, but I was upset that I might get kicked off the basketball team. Basketball means everything to me.*	*I realize that Coach was trying to motivate us to study harder. I should have talked to him after class about what I could do to bring up my grade. Then I would have been calmer and wouldn't have tried to save face with the class. I should never have threatened him with a lawsuit!*
Student: _Coach Carden_ Date: _April 5_	Upon Reflection Date: _April 6_
Description of What Happened	**What I Would Do Differently**
I passed out the tests and talked to the class about their poor performance. Rick was upset and threw his test away. *I was upset because I had planned to review the test and discuss the right answers. He tried to get back at me in front of the class.*	*I should not have passed out the test that way because kids saw each other's papers. I think Rick was embarrassed because one of the cheerleaders saw his 62 percent.* *I shouldn't have made fun of him when he missed the trash with his wadded-up test. I hurt him and he reacted the only way he could—to save face with his peers.*

Figure 9.7

Students with Behavior Problems

- Encourage students who have questions or concerns about assignments or grades to see you privately after class.
- Build in some down time during class while students are working when you are available to discuss problems (especially for students who cannot come in after school).
- Fold over test papers and return them personally to students to preserve confidentiality.
- Don't take the hook. Teenagers are often not in control of their emotions, but teachers should try to be in control of their emotions.

Students with Aggressive Behaviors

Ms. Cox divides the class into cooperative groups and posts the directions for their projects on the board.

Domingo groans when he sees that Jimmy is in his group. "I don't want to work with him," Domingo says to Ms. Cox. "Get him out of my group!"

Ms. Cox walks over to Domingo and asks him, "What is wrong? You know we respect everyone in the class and we try to get along."

"He stole my lunch money," Domingo blurts out. "I don't want to be near that thief!"

"You can't prove that," Jimmy mumbles as he grows more and more red.

"I don't have to prove it," retorts Domingo. "I have three witnesses that saw you take it from my book bag."

Jimmy stands up menacingly and begins walking toward Domingo.

"Sit down," yells Ms. Cox as she runs towards the phone in the room.

Domingo turns to face Jimmy as the rest of the class begins to move their desks away from the impending fight.

Jimmy pulls an Army knife from his pocket and flashes it in front of Domingo's nose. Domingo does not back down and Jimmy inches closer.

One of the boys in the class holds out his foot and trips Jimmy.

Just as Jimmy begins to scuffle with the student who tripped him, the coach in the next room who has heard the scuffle runs into the classroom. He grabs Jimmy, Domingo, and the student who stuck his foot out and hauls them all down to the principal's office.

Solving the Problem

Students who display aggressive behavior are often trying to gain control over their lives. When students constantly utilize anger in an attempt to dominate other students or the group, they are incapable of finding a workable solution to their problems. Their inability to communicate causes them to try to overpower, intimidate, or hurt others. If students are taught to disagree with the idea and not the person, to negotiate, to discuss, and to compromise, aggressive behavior can be prevented. Anger can either be talked out or acted out. When students act out anger, aggression is the result.

> A disinterested student rarely has a satisfying picture of school in his head; perhaps he has the picture of spending his days on the street 'hanging out.' But if his parents are able to force him to go to school, he may choose the angry behavior of disrupting to the extent that he is suspended. Now, out on suspension, he is satisfied. In school he was frustrated and he disrupted to get closer to the picture that he wants. On the street he is in control; in school he has almost no effective control at all (Glasser 1986, p. 53).

Jones and Jones (1998) recommend that teachers do not become emotional or display visible anger when dealing with a student who is demonstrating aggressive behavior. When a teacher begins turning red, speaking louder and faster, and getting upset, the student is so busy thinking about the teacher that he or she cannot think about his or her own mistake or make a new plan of behavior.

Jones and Jones recommend that teachers use the following strategies and procedures (see Figure 9.8) to protect themselves and their students from violent behavior.

Handling Violent Student Behavior

Teachers should:

1. Remain calm and in control.
2. Send a student for assistance (teacher next door, administrator, school security guard).
3. Guard against confrontational methods because they increase chances of violent reactions from students.
4. Acknowledge the student's feelings, offer assistance, suggest alternatives.
5. Talk in a calm, gentle, yet firm, voice.
6. Give the students adequate space.
7. Remove the audience by asking the rest of the class to go to the library or to another teacher's classroom.
8. Continue to talk to the student about resolving the conflict before the administrator comes.

Adapted from Jones and Jones 1998, pp. 287–288. Reprinted with permission.

Figure 9.8

Of course, all the steps listed in Figure 9.8 can help diffuse the immediate aggressive situation, but the next steps involve meeting with the student, and perhaps the counselor and/or the parents. The behavior needs to be analyzed as to what provoked it, and some form of behavioral interventions, checkpoints, or conferences need to be set to monitor the student's ability to prevent future disturbances. In many cases, the aggressive outburst was merely a symptom of a more complex issue that needs to be articulated and addressed before the aggressive behavior stops.

Violent behavior problems cannot be handled with a detention or names on the board. Teachers need to work with students to develop a long-term action plan. When a student uses a weapon or attempts to use a weapon, he or she is usually suspended or expelled, depending upon the school rules. Other aggressive behaviors, however, include students threatening others, using their fists, or using their books or a desk in a violent fashion. The teacher needs to react quickly to protect the other students, and then work toward solving the long-term problem of the student's aggressive behavior when or if the student returns to class. Figure 9.9 shows a sample Action Plan for the scenario described, and a Blackline master at the end of this selection offers a form teachers can use to help their students (see Blackline 9.4).

Other Strategies Teachers Can Use with Students with Aggressive Behaviors

- After the student returns from suspension or expulsion, talk privately with him to find out why he behaves so aggressively with other students. Try to get to the cause of the problem by asking what personal issues may be causing the problem. Perhaps a counselor needs to be involved if the home problems involve abuse or parental problems.
- Call the student's parents and find out if she has displayed any aggressive tendencies at home or in other school situations, discuss possible solutions, and schedule follow-up conferences.
- Talk with the school counselor to see if there are any previous behavior problems on the student's record. See if a special education class or special counseling is warranted.
- Give the student the option of going to the time-out or satellite area to work on his own when the pressure builds. He should be responsible for all work, but he should do it individually, without assistance from the group.
- Set up a verbal or nonverbal signal that gives the student a warning that she is losing control. For example, one hand across another showing she has "crossed the line."
- Review the behaviors of the other students in the class to see if he is particularly aggravated by one of them and is, therefore, acting out because of a personality conflict.

Students with Behavior Problems

Action Plan

Analyze the problem and create an Action Plan for the incident.

Students: *Jimmy, Domingo, Paul*

Problem: *Jimmy pulls an Army knife on another student.*

Quick-Recovery Actions

1. *I can separate the students (unless it poses a danger for me or other students).*
2. *I can call for help (or send a student for help).*
3. *I can talk calmly to Jimmy to see if he'll drop the knife.*
4. *I can tell the rest of the students to leave the classroom (remove the audience).*

Next-Step Actions

1. *Conference with both students to find out what caused the problem.*
2. *It may be better to talk to students separately to get both sides of the story.*
3. *Talk to the boy who tripped Jimmy.*
4. *Find out about the lunch money incident.*
5. *Get separate statements from all students involved.*

Long-Term Solutions

1. *Ask a peer mediator or counselor to mediate the conflict about the lunch money.*
2. *Reteach social skills dealing with conflict resolution to whole class.*
3. *Carefully select groups for a while to avoid personality conflicts.*
4. *Refer Jimmy to counseling when he returns from suspension or expulsion.*

Teacher: *Ms. Cox* Date: *Sept. 25*

Figure 9.9

- Build a personal relationship with the student by talking with her and discovering her special interests.
- Evaluate his academic status to see if he feels inadequate and is resorting to aggressive behavior to compensate for his inability to keep up with the rest of the group.
- Change the cooperative group frequently so she doesn't build up a long-standing feud.
- Have students keep a checklist to keep track of their own antisocial behaviors—conference with them at the end of the period, day, or week about how they did and what strategies could help them.
- Videotape or audiotape a class and play it back to the student to let him see how other people perceive his behavior.
- Have the student keep a journal or log where she writes about how she feels when she is upset or angry.
- Assign him a task in which he will succeed to increase his self-esteem.
- While reviewing social skills, role-play a simulated incident involving an aggressive situation and have a discussion about how students should handle the problem.

Students Who Feel Inadequate

Mr. Williams' world history class is studying Greek mythology. The students all have their books open as Mr. Williams calls on various students to read the myths.

"Jamie, will you please read the myth about Aphrodite and Cupid for the class?" Mr. Williams asks.

Jamie turns three shades of red and starts to read slowly and haltingly.

"Aph-ro-dite was very vain. She spent a lot of time primp-ing and gazing in a mirror. On Mount Olymp-us (pause) she lived in a gold palace with her . . .

"I can't pronounce the next word," Jamie mumbles under her breath.

Students with Behavior Problems

"Protégé," offers Mr. Williams.

"Can somebody else read," begs Jamie. "I don't feel well."

"Sure," Mr. Williams answers. "Lucas, will you please take over where Jamie left off?"

Jamie puts her head down on the desk for the rest of the class.

Solving the Problem

Students often play the "I can't" game because they feel they cannot accomplish a task perfectly. Some "inadequate" students need to realize that it's okay to be imperfect. They can still cooperate with others, perform tasks reasonably well, and produce products that are acceptable.

Dinkmeyer and Losoncy (1980) say that inadequate students often say "I can't" when what they really mean is "I won't." "I can't" is a form of passive resistance, whereas "I won't" is a form of active resistance that usually provokes a power struggle or challenge to teachers. According to Dinkmeyer and Losoncy, "The 'I can't' phrase suggests helplessness and can serve the following purposes:

1. One believes others should serve him or her and puts others in service by proclaiming inadequacy.
2. One believes that he or she is an inadequate person and protects himself or herself from possible failure by 'copping out'—avoiding facing life's challenges.
3. One believes that he or she is unable, helpless, and should be excused from being expected to function" (1980, p. 55–56).

Often students who feel inadequate lack confidence in their ability and perceive life as unfair because they may try very hard, but their efforts still lead to failure. These students become discouraged and develop negative self-concepts. In some cases, these students totally withdraw and give up completely (Dinkmeyer and Losoncy 1980). Teachers often let these quiet and withdrawn students slip through the cracks because they are too busy devoting their attention to the noisier students who are seeking attention or power. Unfortunately,

GUIDEBOOK

the discouraged and inadequate block of students is much larger than most people realize, and these quiet students often become dropout statistics. In more cases than not, the roots of the problem can be traced to learning problems. Students who cannot read would rather refuse to read or appear uninterested rather than read in front of the class and embarrass themselves in front of their peers. Bellanca and Fogarty (1991) offer tactics to help inadequate students feel confident and in control (see Figure 9.10).

Tactics Teachers Can Use with Students Who Feel Inadequate

- Assign tasks that the student can successfully complete.
- Talk with the student to analyze why he or she feels inadequate.
- Pair the inadequate student with another empathetic student who can help.
- Lower the student's anxiety about mistakes.
- De-emphasize grades and emphasize a love of learning.
- Break larger tasks into smaller chunks.
- Encourage-encourage-encourage!
- Remind students of past successes.
- Keep high expectations for all students.
- Use team-building activities to build trust among group members.
- Give extra recognition for individual contributions to the group.
- Arrange for homework buddies so the student gets additional help and support.
- Give positive feedback.
- Give specific praise for an action when appropriate.
- Help the student remediate specific learning deficiencies that may be causing feelings of inadequacy.
- Listen empathetically to the student's concerns, fears, and frustrations.
- Structure highly motivating group activities so the student is working toward a goal.

Adapted from Bellanca and Fogarty 1991. Reprinted with permission.

Figure 9.10

Some students who feel inadequate come to teachers with pessimistic expectations that have been ingrained in them since early childhood. Teachers will not always be able to lift the heavy weight from their shoulders after only one or two conferences. Persistence is the key to helping the student who feels inadequate feel successful, become a valuable member of the group, do well on whole group activities, and succeed on individual tasks. These students try to avoid anything that could cause them to fail; therefore, it's the role of the teacher to structure activities that will make the student succeed, gain confidence, and develop a positive self-concept.

One strategy teachers can use is to read between the lines to determine the real cause of a problem. A student could be acting out or withdrawing to cover a real problem that is causing him or her to feel insecure or inadequate. Sometimes a one-on-one private teacher-student conference can help teachers discover how best to help the student.

The key to effective problem solving in a conference is reflective listening. Teachers who use "closed questions" that call for a "yes-or-no" answer and begin with the word "why" tend to cut off true communication.

Closed Questions

"Closed questions" can sound accusatory, somewhat sarcastic, and negative. They antagonize students and put them on the defensive. The smart responses students sometimes give the teacher are in retaliation for the teacher embarrassing the students in front of their peers. Even if students say nothing or reply courteously, they have suffered humiliation and their self-esteem has been lowered. It is doubtful that "closed questions" will motivate students to shape up. Some sample closed questions are given in Figure 9.11.

Sample Closed Questions

Question: "Are you just going to sit there or are you going to get busy?"

Answer: "Yes, I'm going to sit here—what are you going to do about it?"

Question: "Do you really think you're funny?"

Answer: "Yes, I do think I'm funny!"

Question: "Why don't you stop fooling around and get on task?"

Answer: "Because, I'm not quite finished fooling around yet."

Figure 9.11

Open Questions

"Open questions" invite further conversation and many possible responses. They also help establish a rapport between teacher and student because they convey to the student a sense of caring and fairness (see Figure 9.12).

Sample Open Questions

Question: "Why do you think you get nervous when you read out loud?"

Answer: "I am embarrassed I might make a mistake and the kids might laugh."

Question: "Hmm. How can I help you feel more confident when you read in front of the class?"

Answer: "Maybe you could work with me after school to help me learn to pronounce the words?"

Figure 9.12

As the teacher listens to the student talk about the problem, he or she may want to listen for and draw out the following "subtexts."

- Could it be the student would like other students to notice her more?
- Could it be other students tease her about reading out loud?

Students with Behavior Problems

- Could it be she has a language problem that embarrasses her?

Dreikurs recommends that during such a discussion, teachers look carefully at the student for what he calls a "recognition reflex," or an involuntary sign that the guess is correct. The reflex could be a shift in posture, a change in eye contact, or a nonverbal cue that indicates the underlying reason for the problem. Often, the student is not aware of what the real problem is and it's the teacher's job to bring it to the surface (cited in Dinkmeyer, McKay, and Dinkmeyer 1980, p. 114).

As shown in the focus strategy in Figure 9.13, teachers may want to include parents in the plan for solving the problem and bolstering the student's self-esteem. A Blackline master of a Teacher-Student Conference form teachers can use with their students is at the end of this selection (see Blackline 9.5).

Even though teachers are extremely busy and teach many students each day, the one-on-one conference accomplishes a great deal. First, the teacher devotes individual attention to the student. Second, the teacher can focus on the problem without the distractions of the rest of the class. Third, the teacher gets to know the student on a more personal basis. The interpersonal touch goes a long way in helping students gain confidence and overcome inadequacy.

Other Strategies Teachers Can Use with Students Who Feel Inadequate

- A student may increase his self-esteem by succeeding at an extracurricular activity.
- Work out a secret system with the inadequate student. Promise the student that you will only call on her if you are standing right next to her. That way the student does not have to worry about being called on at other times and can concentrate on the lesson.
- Give the inadequate student a great deal of wait time when you ask questions. Also, try to ask questions you know he can answer to build his confidence.

Teacher-Student Conference

After the teacher asks the student a series of open questions, both the teacher and the student fill out this form.

Student: _Jamie_   Teacher: _Mr. Williams_   Date: _Sept. 9_

Teacher's concern: _I am concerned because you don't participate in class discussions and you always seem to get sick or have some other excuse whenever I call on you in class to read or answer a question._

Student's concern: _I am really shy and I don't like to talk in class because I'm afraid I might say something stupid and the other kids will laugh at me. I also hate to read out loud. I get really nervous and I don't understand one thing I read because I'm thinking about pronouncing things wrong or not knowing the words._

Possible options:

1. _Mr. Williams will not call on Jamie unless she has her hand raised._

2. _Mr. Williams will not call on students to read in front of the whole class. He'll either put students in groups of 2 or 3 to read together or allow them to read silently._

3. _Jamie will go to the reading teacher to get tested to see if she needs extra help._

Parent involvement:
I will have Jamie read out loud to me every night to help her feel more comfortable with pronouncing words and reading out loud. I will also buy some audiotapes of stories for her to listen to as she reads.

Parent's signature: _Mrs. Hansen_

Date of next conference: _Sept. 22_

Figure 9.13

Students with Behavior Problems

- Give specific encouragement for the student's accomplishment. In other words, don't just say "Great speech." Tell the student the speech was great because she used good eye contact, effective gestures, and appropriate humor. Be specific.
- Make sure to allow enough time for each activity. Inadequate students often feel rushed, and they become frustrated when the teacher and the class are moving faster than they are.
- Leave some time between activities so students can make the transition. Inadequate students may also suffer from learning disabilities, and they have a difficult time changing their mindset quickly from one task to another.
- Make sure all the homework assignments are realistic. Do not give excessive amounts of homework because inadequate students get very frustrated when they cannot complete all the work. It takes them longer to complete assignments than other students.
- Do not give new material for homework since students might not understand the new concepts. The homework should be a review of concepts already studied.
- Provide rubrics for all major assignments so that students know the expectations for quality work.

With the strategies outlined in this selection, teachers can provide students who demonstrate behavior problems with the appropriate direction and guidance needed to avoid major classroom and learning disturbances.

REFERENCES

Albert, L. 1989. *A teacher's guide to cooperative discipline: How to manage your classroom and promote self-esteem.* Circle Pines, MN: American Guidance Service.

Bellanca, J., and Fogarty, R. 1991. *Blueprints for thinking in the cooperative classroom.* Arlington Heights, IL: IRI/Skylight Publishing.

Curwin, R. L., and Mendler, A. N. 1988. *Discipline with dignity.* Alexandria, VA: Association for Supervision and Curriculum Development.

Dinkmeyer, D., and Losoncy, L. E. 1980. *The encouragement book. Becoming a positive person.* New York: Prentice-Hall.

Dinkmeyer, D., McKay, G. D., and Dinkmeyer, D., Jr. 1980. *Systematic training for effective teaching.* Circle Pines, MN: American Guidance Service.

Glasser, W. 1986. *Control theory in the classroom.* New York: Harper & Row.

Gough, P. B. 1987. The key to improving schools: An interview with William Glasser. *Phi Delta Kappan* 68(9): 657–658.

Jones, V. F., and Jones, L. S. 1998. *Comprehensive classroom management: Creating communities of support and solving problems,* 5th ed. Boston: Allyn & Bacon.

Kauffman, J. M., Hallahan, D. P., Mostert, M. P., Trent, S.C., and Nuttycombe, D. G. 1993. *Managing classroom behavior: A reflective case-based approach.* Needham Heights, MA: Allyn & Bacon.

Levin, J., and Nolan, J. F. 1996. *Principles of classroom management: A professional decision-making model.* 2d ed. Boston: Allyn & Bacon.

Manning, M. L., and Baruth, L. G. 1995. *Students at risk.* Boston: Allyn & Bacon.

Mendler, A. N. 1997. *Power struggles: Successful techniques for educators.* Rochester, New York: Discipline Associates.

Short, P. M., Short, R. J., and Blanton, C. 1994. *Rethinking student discipline: Alternatives that work.* Thousand Oaks, CA: Corwin Press.

Vaughn, S., Bos, C. S., an Schumm, J. S. 2000. *Teaching exceptional, diverse and at-risk students in the general education classroom.* 2d ed. Boston: Allyn & Bacon.

Six Blackline masters are provided on the pages that follow:

- The Newspaper Model
- Phases of a Power Struggle
- Divided Journal
- Action Plan
- Teacher-Student Conference
- Behavior Problems Problem-Solving Applications

The first five are explained in the selection. The last blackline master is provided so that teachers can use any or all of the strategies in this selection to solve a problem with a student. Protégés can use the blacklines with their students when they encounter behavior problems. Mentors can guide their protégés as they use the blacklines and as they devise ways to deal with students' behavior problems.

The Newspaper Model

Name:_____ Date:_____

Problem: _____

Who	What	When	Where	Why

Write a paragraph describing your view of what happened.

Signed: _____

Have another group member write a paragraph about the situation.

Signed: _____

Phases of a Power Struggle

Explosion

Causes

1. _____
   _____
2. _____
   _____
3. _____
   _____

Cool Down

1. _____
   _____
2. _____
   _____
3. _____
   _____

What the teacher could have done to prevent the problem:

What the student could have done to prevent the problem:

Resolution to problem:

Teacher:_____ Student:_____ Date:_____

Blackline 9.2

Divided Journal

Student:_____ Date:_____	Upon Reflection Date:_____
Description of What Happened	**What I Would Do Differently**
Student:_____ Date:_____	Upon Reflection Date:_____
Description of What Happened	**What I Would Do Differently**

Action Plan

Students:
Problem:

Quick-Recovery Actions

Next-Step Actions

Long-Term Solutions

Teacher:_____   Date:_____

Blackline 9.4

MENTORING

Teacher-Student Conference

Student:_____ Teacher:_____ Date:_____

Teacher's concern:_____
_____
_____
_____

Student's concern:_____
_____
_____
_____
_____

Possible options:

1.   _____
     _____

2.   _____
     _____

3.   _____
     _____

Parent involvement:

Parent's signature:_____

Date of next conference:_____

Blackline 9.5

Bahavior Problems
Problem-Solving Application

Directions: Review the strategies in this selection and brainstorm possible solutions to a real problem you have had with a student.

1. Write a brief description of a student you have taught or are currently teaching who has a behavior problem.

Student's First Name:_____ Age:_____ Grade:_____

Description of Problem

2. Based upon the strategies reviewed in this selection and your own ideas, brainstorm two possible solutions to the problem.

Solution One:

Students with Behavior Problems

Solution Two:

3. Write a reflection about the insights you have gained about the student and the problem.

My Reflection

Signed:_____ Date:_____

Conclusion

"In our efforts to support new teachers, we need to remember to encourage them to hold on tightly to their original passion for teaching. And those among us who still love to teach can light the way by being positive role models and by showing new teachers how we find our own ways to keep teaching meaningful." (Hurst, Reding, as cited in Scherer, p. 223).

Just as the Greek teacher Mentor guided the young Telemachus, today's mentor teachers guide new teachers. In addition to helping the protégés develop the organizational skills to succeed, mentors also act as role models. Mentors "walk the talk" and invite new teachers into their classrooms to observe and discuss pedagogy, strategies, and practical tips they learned throughout their careers. Most importantly, mentors share their passion for teaching with their protégés. Despite all the problems faced in the first few years, new teachers can not only survive but also flourish if they are committed to the profession and the students they teach.

The most important role a mentor can play is cheerleader—mentors help keep the love of teaching a major focus throughout the journey. Mentors who share a love of teaching and learning with their protégés can meet and overcome any challenges because they work as a team. Together, the mentor/protégé team share a love of teaching and find new ways to keep teaching both meaningful and fulfilling.

REFERENCES

Hurst, B. and G. Reding as cited in Scherer, ed. 1999. "Helping New Teachers Keep the Light in Their Eyes." In *A Better Beginning: Supporting and Mentoring New Teachers*. Alexandria, VA: Association for the Supervision of Curriculum Development.

Index

SkyLight Professional Development